Country Towns of
WISCONSIN

Country Towns of
WISCONSIN

Charming Small Towns and Villages to Explore

Ann Hattes

COUNTRY ROADS PRESS

NTC/Contemporary Publishing Group

Library of Congress Cataloging-in-Publication Data

Hattes, Ann.
    Country Towns of Wisconsin : charming small towns and villages
to explore / Ann Hattes.
        p.   cm. — (Country towns)
    Includes index.
    ISBN 1-56626-148-1
    1. Wisconsin—Guidebooks.   2. Cities and towns—Wisconsin—
Guidebooks.   3. Automobile travel—Wisconsin—Guidebooks.
4. Wisconsin—History, Local.   I. Title.   II. Series.
F579.3.H38   1999
917.7504'43—dc21   98-31297
                                                                   CIP

Cover and interior design by Nick Panos
Cover and interior illustrations and map copyright © Kathleen O'Malley
Picture research by Elizabeth Broadrup Lieberman
Typesetting by VARDA Graphics, Inc.

Published by Country Roads Press
A division of NTC/Contemporary Publishing Group, Inc.
4255 West Touhy Avenue, Lincolnwood (Chicago), Illinois 60646-1975 U.S.A.
Copyright © 1999 by Ann Hattes
Printed in the United States of America
International Standard Book Number: 1-56626-148-1
99 00 01 02 03 04 ML 18 17 16 15 14 13 12 11 10 9 8 7 6 5 4 3 2 1

To Neil

Helpmate on the Information Highway
Soulmate on the Road of Life

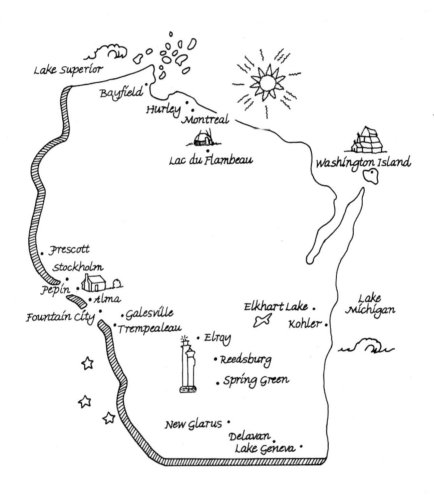

Lake Superior

Bayfield

Hurley

Montreal

Lac du Flambeau

Washington Island

Prescott

Stockholm

Pepin

Alma

Fountain City

Galesville

Trempealeau

Elkhart Lake

Kohler

Lake Michigan

Elroy

Reedsburg

Spring Green

New Glarus

Delavan

Lake Geneva

CONTENTS

INTRODUCTION

Wisconsin is full of surprises: the House on the Rock and a Rock in the House. Site of the world's first auto race and Kohler's great wall of china. Birthplace of Laura Ingalls Wilder, the snowmobile, and more than one hundred circuses. Taliesin and Waswagoning. Home today to a Chinese princess and former Playboy bunny, it once shaped the fate of empires—with beaver furs!

Thanks to my parents who gave me wanderlust. Thanks to my family for abiding my absences as I crisscrossed the state meeting new friends, all of whom gave generously of their time and expertise. Thanks too, to Virginia Duncan, Gary Knowles, Laughlin Constable Inc., the Wisconsin Division of Tourism, local convention bureaus and chambers of commerce for suggestions made and doors opened. Apologies to all the towns that couldn't be included in this volume.

From Mississippi River towns to former lumber and mining towns deep in the north woods to rural Washington Island at "Death's Door," I discovered small-town "can-do" spirit where volunteerism is rampant and retirees rarely retire. Surrounding these country towns I found a John Muir landscape of over ten thousand lakes, millions of acres of forest, 60 state parks, and thousands of miles of multipurpose trails.

Muir, the world-famous naturalist who spent his formative years in Wisconsin, penned these words: "Everybody needs beauty as well as bread; places to play in and places to pray in, where nature may heal and cheer, and give strength to body and soul alike." Wisconsin, with its rural charms, is such a place.

Country Towns of
WISCONSIN

1

SPRING GREEN

WRIGHT IN WISCONSIN

Spring Green nestles in a broad valley of low hills where mists rising from the nearby Wisconsin River create what Frank Lloyd Wright's architecture apprentices call the "Japanese print morning." Wright, who was born and grew up in the area, wrote of being cradled by these gentle hills. Eventually he built his home and studio here, calling it Taliesin (pronounced Tally-es-sin) which means "shining brow" in Welsh. At Taliesin, Wright entertained artists and architects, students and monarchs from around the world, and began the drawings for what would later become Tokyo's Imperial Hotel and New York's Guggenheim Museum.

Wright believed a house should be part of a hill, never something on it. Visitors taking the Taliesin walking tour approach his house from below the hill, having no idea where it is or how close they are until they're suddenly upon it. Redesigned and rebuilt several times by Wright's students through the years, Taliesin is constructed of materials found near the site. The house lies close to the ground with low eaves reaching out over an enclosed walled garden. Sitting on a farm once owned by his ancestors, it's Wright's autobiography in wood and stone.

Known around the world for "breaking the box" and creating "organic" architecture, Wright blended buildings with their surroundings, drawing inspiration from their settings. This idea of seamless integration with the environment carried over into daily life; Taliesin had a farm where fellowship students grew their own food, raised their own animals, and cooked their own meals. Though the farm is no longer operative, the barn and dairy buildings still stand. Taliesin senior fellows and apprentices continue to share in the tradition of taking turns cooking and serving meals, doing the dishes, and arranging and decorating the communal dining room.

Throughout his career, which spanned seven decades, Wright always said nature was the great architect. "How did nature do it? How can we do it?" he would ask. Thus, from a close observation of the structure of a cactus, the strong but slender pillars of reinforced concrete were born.

In the village of Spring Green, Wright is often remembered as a proud eccentric striding along with a walking stick, black cape billowing behind him, fully personifying the family motto, "Truth Against the World." Wright's unconventional decision to live openly with his mistress set him apart from the residents of this conservative rural community. "I determined early in life that I'd have to choose between honest arrogance and hypocritical humility. I chose the former and have seen no reason to change," he said.

Wright's shadow still lingers in Spring Green, where the bank might easily double as a flying saucer in a Hollywood set. The two bank buildings (1972 and 1983), both on Jefferson Street, and St. John's Catholic Church (1990) on Daley Street, were designed by William Wesley Peters, whom Wright referred to as his "right bower." Peters, Wright's son-in-law, came from MIT to join the Taliesin Fellowship when it began in 1932, staying until his death in 1991.

Local lodging like the Prairie House Motel, Usonian Inn, and Round Barn Lodge, all on Highway 14 just north of town, were designed by former Wright students still living in the area. The dome-shaped Round Barn restaurant started in 1904 as a round dairy barn housing 44 head of Holsteins. The Usonian Inn, built in 1950, was the first motel in the area.

Spring Green itself began with the coming of the railroad in 1856. Two converted cheese warehouses, a railway station/bank, and a transformed lumber yard along the railroad tracks in the center of town testify to the village's past.

At the Washington Street studio and gallery of papermaker/printmaker Jura Silverman, look for evidence of the old exhaust system that carried off the paraffin fumes from the large cheese-dipping vat below. Between the displays of artwork, all by Wisconsin artists, see gouges on the floor made by crate nails as boxes were shoved across what was formerly a Borden Company warehouse.

"There's no place quite like Spring Green—so much culture, yet very rural," states Cease Grinwald, past proprietress of one of several shops at Lexington Station along the tracks. "There's so much creativity, energy, and spirituality here. People are called here and become part of the fabric of the community." Relocated to the area herself, Grinwald encouraged adding performing artists to Spring Green's annual Country Christmas Festival of the Arts, celebrated on December weekends. The village also hosts an art fair attracting artists and craftspeople from throughout the Midwest for one weekend every June.

Since 1980, American Players Theatre (APT) has offered Shakespeare, Marlowe, Molière, Chekhov, Ibsen, and Wilder in an outdoor wooded setting, from June to October. Recognized as one of the nation's top repertory companies, APT presents the classics with bug spray and stars, sometimes even raindrops.

Frank Lloyd Wright regularly gathered his students together in his home on Sunday nights for a dinner followed by musical concerts. He believed that art cannot be taught; rather, an

atmosphere has to be created in which it can grow. In this tradition, local residents present concerts every other Monday in
July and August in the small Unity Chapel, built by Wright's
mother's Lloyd-Jones family in 1886. Look for it near the junc-
tion of Highway 23 and County Highway T four miles south
of Spring Green.

Walk into the grove of trees surrounding the chapel to see
Wright's original grave. (He's since been moved to Arizona
at the request of his third wife.) Look too for the graves of
Wright's mistress, her 11-year-old daughter, and 8-year-old
son who were hacked to death, along with four other people,
by a servant under circumstances still shrouded in mystery.
Wright's granddaughter, actress Anne Baxter, is buried here
as well.

John Korb, formerly a concierge at the nearby Springs Golf
Club Resort, is a walking encyclopedia on Wright, Spring
Green, and its environs, gladly sharing his wide-ranging
knowledge with guests. He'll tell you that Wright's son John
created and patented Lincoln Logs. Korb also talks of the
two Svetlanas, both originally from Georgia in the Crimea.
The second Svetlana was none other than Joseph Stalin's
daughter.

Not far from the chapel at the intersection of Route 23 and
County Highway C, is the Frank Lloyd Wright Visitors Center in Riverview Terrace, the only restaurant ever designed by
Wright. Overlooking a bend in the Wisconsin River, the 300-
foot-long building, the starting point for all tours of Taliesin,
uses steel trusses recycled from a World War II aircraft carrier. The center houses exhibits, an extensive bookstore and
gift shop, plus a café that's open during tourist season.

For an in-depth view of the 20th century's architectural
giant, join one of several tours of the 600-acre estate which
are offered from May through October. The tour program
varies from year to year, so it's best to call ahead for information, brochures, and reservations. Taliesin, declared a

Taliesin Tower

National Historic Landmark in 1976, encompasses Wright's personal residence, the entire 600-acre property, and other buildings of Wright's design: Hillside Home School (1902);

Midway Farm (1930s and 1940s); Tan-y-deri house (1907); and the Romeo and Juliet Windmill (1897), diamond and octagon forms embracing each other. No other location embodies such a complete example of Wright's work through the years.

Just below the visitor center, on the other side of County Highway C, the Wisconsin River flows quietly by. In warm weather, canoeists leisurely paddle these gentle waters, wending between sandbars populated with picnickers and campers. Back in the mid-1800s, in contrast to today's pastoral setting, raftsmen maneuvered millions of board feet down these same waters. With oars 18 feet long, they manned fleets of 12 to 14 log rafts to sawmills along the shores. Whiskey Jack, a Paul Bunyon counterpart, was said to be seven feet tall, with the strength of Samson.

Until the recent Wright renaissance, Spring Green was known not for one of the world's great architects, but for "the Grand Canyon of road attractions," the House on the Rock (open late March to October and late November to early January). Originally built as a weekend retreat atop a 60-foot chimney rock, it attracted attention because of its location. Recently, the House on the Rock was voted one of the top 10 devotional shrines in the world by subscribers to America Online.

Alex J. Jordan, the house's reticent builder, explained it this way in a Kimberly-Clark interview: "At first we used to picnic on the rock . . . a little steak, a small hibachi. . . . When the farmer asked me what I was doing, I said how I admired the rock. . . . I leased it . . . gave him $20 to picnic on it. . . .

"I worked on it for years pretty much alone . . . carried up the cement, carried up the sand, carried up the water and timbers. . . . There was never a master plan—it just developed as I went along."

Passersby stopped and asked Jordan for tours and Madison elite rented the retreat for parties. Though at first Jordan charged a fee to discourage visitors, he soon realized he had a hit in the making. He officially opened the House on the Rock to the public in 1961, billing it as "Wisconsin's No. 1 tourist attraction."

Through the years, visitors have commented on the similarity between Wright's Taliesin and Jordan's dream house. In both homes, the land, shrubs, buildings, and furnishings seem to blend together as a whole. However, John Korb says that Jordan and Wright never met. Jordan himself claimed he first saw Taliesin long after he had finished his own design.

As more and more visitors trekked to his famous house, Jordan's fertile imagination created a vast labyrinth of warehouse-sized structures filled with entertainment to satisfy the public: the world's largest carousel; automated music machines, including the world's only mechanically operated symphony orchestra; entire buildings devoted to theater organs, dollhouses, miniature circuses, weapons, and armor. The actual house now accounts for only 5 percent of the House on the Rock tour, leading the way to the Streets of Yesterday and marvels like the Franz Josef music machine and the Great Carved Tusk of Ranchipur.

Jam-packed with real antiques and art, plus hundreds of genuine fakes, the House on the Rock is pure and simple show business. Though Jordan died in 1989, the House on the Rock continues to stand as a memorial to his life. Baffling the imagination and defying all definition, the House on the Rock has to be experienced to be believed. Even then, it's still not quite believable.

Traveling the seven miles from the House on the Rock back to Spring Green along Highway 23, you'll pass the Wyoming Valley Elementary School (1957), the only Wright-designed public school in the country. Privately owned, it's no longer in use and is not open to the public.

Back in town on Highway 23, turn left just across the railroad tracks. Go down the alley one block to the Spring Green

Café and General Store. This once rural Wisconsin cheese co-op is now a natural foods grocery and village gathering spot. Stop for soup, a sandwich, and a salad, or pick up supplies for a picnic at nearby Tower Hill State Park (open May through October). The park, just outside town on County Highway C, boasts one of the world's few remaining shot towers. In the 1840s, molten lead was poured down the 120-foot shaft to make lead shot. Take along a flashlight if you're planning to climb the dark interior for a panoramic view of the rolling wooded landscape.

Spring Green makes an ideal springboard for a day of sightseeing, bike riding, canoeing, or hiking. Seven miles to the north in Plain is the small, family-owned Cedar Grove Cheese Factory (open year-round). Seventeen miles west on Highway 14 in Richland Center, Wright's birthplace, is the massive, four-story A. D. German Warehouse (open June through October; other times by appointment) designed by the architect in 1915. The warehouse is one of eight Wright sites open to the public in Wisconsin and unified through a Heritage Tourism Initiative that pairs the historic preservation community and the tourism industry.

At the end of the day in Spring Green, retire to one of several cozy B&Bs or collapse in a two-room suite at the Taliesin-inspired Springs Golf Club Resort where the interior decor, from bedspreads to draperies, is based on graphic designs by Wright. In the resort's dining room, Grille on the Green, sample American regional cuisine and unique vegetarian fare in the tradition of Wright-inspired "organic" dining.

In winter, you can cross-country ski or snowshoe at nearby Governor Dodge State Park or at The Springs Golf Club Resort. You can even ski for chocolate at the resort during Valentine season, stopping at food oases to replace burned calories with sweet creations. For indoor activity any time of the year, rejuvenate in luxury at The Springs' fitness center.

Spring Green, which successfully blends architecture, art, and nature into one community, fulfills Wright's dream for a rural alternative to urban life. Virginia Duncan, a member of Wisconsin's Governor's Council on Tourism, sums up the town this way: "It's a triumphant combination of the classics (American Players Theatre), Frank Lloyd Wright, and a premier golf resort."

The village is especially inviting at the end of a long winter when color comes early to the nearby south-facing hollows. Then visitors find, just as the resident who named the town did, true delight in Spring Green!

Places to See, Eat, and Stay

Spring Green Chamber of Commerce: (608) 588-2042.

Taliesin: (608) 588-7900.

House on the Rock: (608) 935-3639.

American Players Theatre: (608) 588-7401.

The Springs Golf Club Resort: (608) 588-7000; (800) 822-7774.

2

ELROY AND REEDSBURG

RAILS TO TRAILS AND NORMAN ROCKWELL

W isconsin's folksy Governor Tommy Thompson describes his hometown as so small that when you dial
a wrong number you end up in a 30-minute conversation.
(Only time will tell if Elroy is a northern counterpoint to
Plains, Georgia, or Hope, Arkansas.) Thompson, who has
always lived in Elroy, never misses voting there. Active in
school extracurricular activities, he often helped out in his
father's combination grocery store and gas station. "One of
Tommy's big jobs when he was quite small was to clean up
and polish eggs when local farmers would bring them in,"
says lifelong Elroy resident Tilmar Roalkvam, who worked
part-time for the governor's dad. Roalkvam was a rural letter carrier like Tommy's grandpa.

Governor Thompson is Elroy's most famous resident,
unless you count Knut Hamsun, a Norwegian Nobel Prize–
winning author who lived in town for awhile as a young man

and then returned to his homeland. Hamsun worked in the local printing office and, while staying in the local hotel, he painted rosemaling—highly stylized floral designs—on the ceiling and walls, according to Roalkvam. The hotel has since been torn down, but Hamsun's experiences in the New World as a farm laborer and Chicago streetcar conductor are included in his novels. Following World War II, Hamsun was charged with treasonable behavior, though eventually the charges were dropped due to his advanced age.

The first settlement in 1851, just to the north of the present boundaries of Elroy, was known as Fowler's Prairie. But newcomers chose to settle closer to the narrowing of the Baraboo River, an optimal location for a dam. A gristmill soon replaced the existing sawmill, so area farmers didn't need to make the day-long trek to the mill at Lemonweir. The trip often required an overnight stay as well. With the Elroy gristmill attracting other businesses, more people moved in.

Leroy was suggested as a name for the growing settlement by an early resident who had moved from a town of that name in New York. When it turned out that there already was a Leroy, Wisconsin, the founder's daughter suggested reversing the first two letters, and Elroy was born.

News of the railroad coming to town caused a boom. By August 1872, when the first train arrived in Elroy, the hamlet had doubled in size. By 1879, it had incorporated as a village and, by 1885, as a city. It continued to grow, with the population reaching over 2,000 in 1905. Today, though still nominally a city, Elroy has shrunk in size to well below that number.

"No train ever went through Elroy without stopping," explains Tilmar Roalkvam, "because Elroy is halfway between Chicago and Minneapolis. We had a big depot here where the trains had to be serviced. Those from the south would split up, one part going on the Omaha Road and the other on the

Northwestern. When coming from either Minneapolis or Rapid City, South Dakota, they would merge into one train south from here to Chicago."

Elroy's large railroad station became its fire station in 1985. "From the outside," says Roalkvam, "it still looks like a depot."

When the direct rail line between Milwaukee and the Twin Cities was built in 1910, Elroy declined, the decline continuing until there were no more tracks. Today the town claims fame as being the very first community with a rail-to-trail ecohighway—"the granddaddy of them all," according to Roalkvam.

The Elroy-Sparta Recreational Trail, a converted rail bed, was the first trail of its kind in the United States to be designated a National Recreation Trail by the U.S. Department of Interior. Here, where steam locomotives used to haul grain, livestock, and passengers and where Harry Truman passed on his 1948 whistle-stop campaign, upward of 80,000 people a year now come to bicycle, hike, and snowmobile. Those who, for unknown reasons, like to irk Governor Thompson, reverse the order and call this historic trail the Sparta-Elroy Trail. The Elroy-Sparta Trail is ranked among the nation's top three best trails by *Bicycling* magazine.

The conversion from rail to trail occurred surprisingly quickly, considering the slow pace of the rest of the country to engage in similar projects. After rail service to Elroy ended in 1964, the Wisconsin Department of Natural Resources established the trail the following year, opening it to the public in 1967. Nineteen years later, in 1986, when the national Rails-to-Trails Conservancy was established, there were only 100 rail-trails open in the country, with another 90 projects underway.

Rail beds, with their gentle grades and easy access, make ideal routes for leisurely rides in the countryside, especially for families and beginning riders. With no traffic and no need to check a map, it's even possible to ride double and chat while pedaling. In winter, snowmobiles use the route.

The 33-mile Elroy-Sparta Recreational Trail boasts three tunnels built in 1873 by the Chicago Northwestern Railroad. From one-quarter to three-quarters of a mile in length, they are damp and dark, so take along a flashlight and a jacket. Though the headquarters for the trail is in a restored railroad depot in Wilton, about midway to Sparta, Elroy Commons is "where the trails meet." Here, energetic cyclers connect with the 400 State Trail and the Omaha Trail.

At the Commons, often the scene of Saturday night entertainment during the summer, two large canopies provide a rest area with picnic tables. Bikes, trail passes, and souvenirs are available, as are showers, restrooms, and phones. Staff provide answers to questions about facilities along the trails, such as the park named after Governor Thompson's father where only hikers and bikers are allowed. Both the trail and the Commons are open May 1 to October 31.

For the "biggest little fair in the state," be in Elroy's Schultz Park the last weekend in July. "It's not a county fair," explains Tilmar Roalkvam. "It's one of a very few that are called 'district' fairs."

But, why hold a district fair in Elroy for almost a hundred years—since 1897, in fact? "There's quite a large hill between Elroy and the county seat about 12 miles from here," says Roalkvam. "It was awfully hard for Elroy people to go over the hill to get to Mauston and vice versa, so we set up our own fair. We have more animals than at the Juneau County Fair, and we always have a big country singer, someone like Louise Mandrell or Mark Collie."

The DogHouse Bar, the Twins' beauty salon, a small museum, and a 1907 Carnegie library can all be found in downtown Elroy. So, too, can the classic car factory, Duesenberg Motors Precision Classic, Inc. at 1 Heritage Lane.

Here, a handful of employees create such $160,000 wonders as the Botash Speedster, Royalton, Murphy Roadster, and Torpedo Pieton. For golfers who like to collect cars, they make scaled-down versions as golf carts. Despite the price, there continues to be a waiting list for these reproductions in all sizes.

Those continuing on through Elroy by pedal power have a choice of the 12.5-mile scenic Omaha Trail or the 22-mile 400 State Trail. The Omaha, established by Juneau County, passes through an 875-foot tunnel about halfway to its destination of Camp Douglas, once the site of a woodcutting camp that was essential in providing firewood to keep train steam boilers running for Chicago, Milwaukee, and St. Paul. Today it's home to the Wisconsin National Guard. Take a self-guided walking/driving tour of the post, including a stop at the museum housed in an 1890s log building.

The 400 State Trail, like the Elroy-Sparta, is on a former railroad right-of-way, following somewhat hilly terrain along the Baraboo River en route to Reedsburg. A bridle path parallels the seven-mile stretch from Wonewoc to La Valle.

Reedsburg is part of the Wisconsin Bikeway, a 300-mile route leading from La Crosse to Kenosha, the first statewide bicycle route in the United States. A country town experiencing a boom, Reedsburg sits near the state's busiest tourist area, only minutes from the Dells, Devil's Lake and Mirror Lake State Parks, Baraboo, and the Ho-Chunk Golden Nickel Casino operated by the Winnebago tribe. Deer hunters take note. Reedsburg is within the top five counties in the state for deer harvest.

Cartoonist Clare A. Briggs, born and raised in Reedsburg, made this country town's "Old Swimming Hole" and his childhood friend "Skinny" famous. Best remembered for titles like "When a Feller Needs a Friend," and "Ain't It a Grand and Glorious Feelin'?" Briggs gained national recognition while working for the *New York Herald Tribune*. While living in New York, he befriended Norman Rockwell. A 1914 Briggs cartoon possibly even inspired a 1927 *Saturday Evening Post* magazine cover by Rockwell.

A trip to Reedsburg is not complete without a visit to the Museum of Norman Rockwell Art. Rockwell seemed to epitomize country town life in his realistic and homey magazine cover art for the *Saturday Evening Post* and other magazines. What more appropriate image, for example, than "The Butter Girl" to honor Reedsburg, the Butter Capital of America? For several years running, Wisconsin Dairies of Reedsburg produced more butter than anywhere else in the nation, a feat still commemorated with an annual Butter Festival the third weekend in June. And despite the dangers of cholesterol we've all heard about, Culver's, a local fast-food spot, specializes in butter burgers and frozen custard.

Rockwell spent his childhood summers with his family in rural New York, an area known for its dairy farming as Wisconsin is. Though he never visited Reedsburg, he did visit northwestern Wisconsin not too far from the Twin Cities. While illustrating for Brown & Bigelow, he spent many nights at the Hudson home of the company's vice-president, Robert Henderson.

Rockwell's original paintings are in the Norman Rockwell Museum in Stockbridge, Massachusetts, where he had his studio for many years. It is mainly through magazine covers and advertisements, however, that Americans came to know this illustrator as an "artist of the people." In Reedsburg's museum, that is how Rockwell is presented. The largest collection of its kind open to the public, it spans 65 years of creativity by the artist.

Viewers delight in slices of Americana, from pre–World War I to modern-day rock stars, often seeing themselves reflected in the thousands of original magazine covers, calendars, and story illustrations on display. All 323 *Saturday Evening Post* covers are here, along with 54 *Literary Digest* covers, 32 rare *Country Gentlemen* covers, 24 almost unknown covers of *Life*, plus the Four Freedoms and the Boy Scout series. Browsers and buyers discover a large selection of framed and unframed prints at the museum. It's open year-round, but call ahead in winter to double-check the schedule.

While downtown Reedsburg is somewhat reminiscent of Rockwell's paintings, perhaps no Wisconsin town is more Rockwellesque than Cedarburg north of Milwaukee. Famous for its 19th-century stone houses, mills, inns, churches, Victorian homes, and antique shops, its successful efforts at preservation have helped it grow beyond a country town, to what some might call a "country burb." Nevertheless, its quaintness and uniqueness continue to charm residents and visitors alike, making it a popular year-round country getaway destination. For an old-fashioned Christmas straight out of a Norman Rockwell painting, Cedarburg can't be beat.

For a sense of Reedsburg as it used to be about a hundred years ago, stop just east of town on Highway 33 at the Reedsburg Area Historical Society. Here members show off log homes, a church, a blacksmith shop, and a school (all from the 1890s) during the summer on Saturdays and Sundays, 1 P.M. to 4 P.M.

Also on Highway 33 on the east side of town, visitors will discover the Liberty Flag & Specialty Company showroom with flags for every holiday and celebration.

Wisconsin, says a state tourism ad, "is a place where people still wave to passing neighbors . . . where people have taken everyday living and made it an art form. . . . Some people own Rockwell paintings. We live in them." This is certainly true for Reedsburg.

Places to See, Eat, and Stay

Elroy Commons: (608) GO-2-BIKE (462-2453).

Elroy-Sparta Recreational Trail: (608) 337-4775.

Reedsburg Chamber of Commerce: (608) 524-2850; (800) 844-3507.

Museum of Norman Rockwell Art: (608) 524-2123.

Liberty Flag & Specialty Company: (608) 524-2834; (800) 274-7001.

3
NEW GLARUS

HEIDI, WILHELM TELL, AND
FLAVORS OF SWITZERLAND

Sitting on the enclosed balcony of the New Glarus Hotel, dining on cheese fondue with polka music playing in the background, it's easy to imagine this as Glarus, Switzerland. All around are reminders of the old country—red geraniums cascading from window boxes of chalet-style homes; colorful canton shields and Swiss flags; conversations sprinkled with German Swiss dialect; *kalberwurst* and *landjaeger* at the butcher shop; *burebrot* and *schweizerbrot* at the bakery. But this is New Glarus, America's Little Switzerland, in south central Wisconsin, a two-and-a-half-hour drive from Chicago.

The venture started back in Switzerland in the 1840s, with the impact of the Industrial Revolution. The printing of cloth, a task that Glarus citizens had been doing by hand, became mechanized, resulting in the loss of jobs and a depressed economy. The Emigration Society of the Canton Glarus stepped in, sending two scouts ahead to the United States to purchase land for a Swiss settlement and promising financial aid to any family wishing to attempt the journey.

Nicholas Duerst and Fridolin Streiff had some requirements to meet as they searched for the perfect spot in America: 1,200 acres at $1.25 per acre, the standard price in the new nation at the time; a plentiful supply of timber and water; and good soil for farming. After researching several locations, they picked the Sugar River Valley with its rolling hills, virgin forests, numerous streams, and rich black soil.

In April 1845, 193 people set out from Glarus, crossing the ocean by ship, then the new continent by rail, canal boat, and barge. Only 108 reached their final destination on August 15, 1845. They created a crude shelter against the Wisconsin winter by burrowing into the hillside, using boards, hay, and boughs to enclose the exposed sides.

Food was scarce, though fish was plentiful in the nearby river. Many would have starved during the first winter had it not been for a $1,000 gift sent from the canton (state) of Glarus. A close bond between the old country and the new continues to this day. The Glarus and New Glarus museums exchange exhibits. Families and friends visit each other, renewing ties and joining in festive community celebrations.

Hotelier Hans Lenzlinger, owner of the New Glarus Hotel, settled here a little over 25 years ago. He remembers well learning about New Glarus in school back in Switzerland. He also has vivid memories of listening to a radio program on Swiss radio about the emigration to New Glarus. "I'm a fairly newcomer here," comments Hans, "but nobody knows New Glarus history in more detail than Elda."

Elda Schiesser's Swiss roots run deep in New Glarus. Most of her relatives came from Glarus, though they weren't part of the initial group of settlers. "My dad came to America from Berne," explains Elda. "He came as a boy at the age of six, with his mother who had nine sons and no husband. I call that women's lib."

New Glarus is especially known for its festivals when the entire community shares its Swiss traditions with visitors. In January a huge bonfire, accompanied by Swiss songs, yodeling, and alphorns, symbolically represents the burning of winter. The first weekend in June brings a Polkafest, followed by a Heidi Festival the last weekend of June. Volksfest, always the first Sunday in August, celebrates Swiss Independence Day.

The Wilhelm Tell Festival, a Labor Day tradition since 1938, is performed in German (Sunday) and English (Saturday and Monday) in an outdoor setting, with a cast of hundreds, plus goats, cows, and horses. New Glarus is the only location in the world to have an English-language Tell drama and the only place outside Switzerland where the drama is presented. The three-and-a-half-hour presentation of Schiller's classic drama depicts Switzerland's struggle for independence in 1291.

Visit the Swiss Village Museum for a historical perspective on this unique Swiss settlement which began as a foreign government–sponsored colony. The museum's 13 buildings and hall of history are at the top of the hill (open daily, May 1 to October 31, 9 A.M.–4:30 P.M.). Here attention focuses on the crude lifestyle experienced by the early colonists during their first years in this vast land. Remember that the entire Swiss nation is only about one quarter the size of Wisconsin. Back in Switzerland, before they left, each family possessed only about 150 to 650 square yards of earth. Contrast this with that first spring when land was apportioned into 20-acre lots, with each of the 60 immigrant families also having common access to the timber lot.

Tour the nearby Chalet of the Golden Fleece (open daily, May 1 to October 31, 10 A.M.–4:30 P.M.), an authentic copy of a Swiss Bernese mountain chalet, displaying treasures from around the world.

"Swiss visitors to New Glarus hear more Swiss music on a weekend here than they would in Switzerland. And they have more Swiss food, too. At home, they'd probably go out to a Chinese restaurant!" So says Nancy Potter, owner of the New Glarus Bakery & Tea Room. "I think of this as a dinosaur business. When I first started here over 15 years ago, there were five bakeries within a radius of 20 miles and now there's only one. The bakery business is labor-intensive. This one survives because it fills a unique niche. It's an artisan bakery."

The New Glarus Bakery bakes bread using steam to create Swiss-style bread and rolls—light on the inside with a hard and crunchy crust. "Fifty years ago in America everybody used steam, but it's too high maintenance today. With steam, the oven rusts. We have to clean and oil it every day," explaines Potter.

Everything at the bakery is made from scratch, including the puff pastry and doughnuts. The sourdough, white, rye, and pumpernickel breads are all made from a long fermentation. "Most bakeries use a type of bread machine dough. It's such a short time, the flavors don't have time to develop and that's the difference," Potter says. "Our breads are denser, heavier. The sourdough preferred out in San Francisco has more holes and is lighter. For us here, that's considered a day when the bread didn't turn out!"

The bakery specializes in Swiss breads and German-style pastries like fruit tortes. In addition to a good local following, Potter knows she has many repeat customers who aren't really tourists, but who come from out of town to buy 10 or 12 loaves of bread to stock in the freezer. "A lot of people come to New Glarus for food," she summarizes. "They go out to the Prima Käse for cheese, stop by the New Glarus Brewing Co. for beer, then go to Ruef's for sausage and the bakery for bread. There are not many places where you have a butcher shop and a bakery in one town. And in New Glarus everything—bread, beer, cheese, and sausage—is made on the spot."

The coarse raisin pumpernickel is popular, as are squares of *Beinenstich Kuchen* (bee stings). A standard in every German bakery, bee stings are made from a sweet dough, split and filled with a light buttercream filling, then topped off with a honey almond glaze. Though it sounds heavy, it isn't. It's pure ambrosia. In Europe, this cake is often enjoyed with afternoon coffee.

Mostly the New Glarus Bakery is known for its nearly two-pound Christmas stollen, a moist, dense, yeast loaf with almonds, marzipan, and raisins. Thousands are mail-ordered all around the country every holiday season in November and December.

For serious sampling at breakfast, lunch, or in between, climb the stairs to the Tea Room on the second floor above the bakery. Like scones? Try the fat rascal. Though you'll find no made-to-order eggs or pancakes here, there is a breakfast quiche and also a breakfast croissant with ham, cheese, and tomato. The Tea Room is especially popular for late afternoon dessert after a day of sightseeing and shopping.

Just a few doors away is Ruef's Meat Market, billed as "The Wurst Store in New Glarus." Willy Ruef, a Swiss native, smokes meats and stuffs fresh sausages, using only natural casings. His store is known mostly for *kalberwurst,* a Swiss veal sausage with whole milk and crackers added; and *landjaeger,* a moist and flavorful Swiss-style jerky that is cured, smoked, and then dried. *Kalberwurst,* a favorite for Swiss Sunday dinners and holidays, is hard to find, but its delicate flavor makes it a food fit for a *Burgermeister.* Ruef's beef and pork stick is a true *landjaeger,* as he still uses the old recipe. No refrigeration is needed, which makes it popular for backpacking, biking, fishing, or just plain snacking.

Ruef, who custom-smokes meat, confides that you never stop learning the trade. He has two smokers: the old-fashioned brick-lined, closetlike shaft, blackened with creosote from the smoke; and an ultramodern stainless steel contrap-

tion with thermometers and automatic graph-
ing charts to prove to the government he has
brought the product up to the right tempera-
ture. Many items he still prefers to do the old-
fashioned way, switching to the 20th-century
model only for the required cooking process.

Don't forget the cheese to go with the brats,
sausages, and beer. New Glarus sits right in the
middle of cheese country, with Monroe County
producing about 40 percent of the nation's total each year.
Whatever your tastes—Asiago, Butterkase, Havarti, Muen-
ster, Gouda, sweet Swiss, cheddar curd, even Limburger—
you'll find it here.

Born on a farm nearby, Elda Schiesser used to make costumes for the Tell pageant. For 22 years she volunteered at
the Swiss Historical Village, serving as a guide, a researcher,
and a member of the board of directors. For the 150th anniversary celebration of the New Glarus settlement, she and
her daughter compiled a year-by-year chronology, "The
Swiss Endure: 1845–1995."

Currently, however, Schiesser spends as much time as possible on her Alpine paper cuttings, or *scherenschnitte*. She
became interested in paper cutting when, back in 1962, she
purchased a cutting by Walter Von Guten, a Swiss native
who took part in one of the first New Glarus Wilhelm Tell
art fairs. Now in her early seventies, she taught herself the
folk art from two books and special scissors she purchased
in Switzerland in 1985. "I just started because I thought it
was a Swiss folk art that New Glarus should have and nobody
else was doing it," she comments matter-of-factly.

The technique of *scherenschnitte* involves cutting a contin-
uous design from one piece of paper. Only symmetric designs are created by folding the paper. Schiesser uses the true
Swiss form of black on white, though she sometimes does
brown on white or white on black, especially for custom

orders. She creates her designs by working out the individual parts of a particular work, then maneuvering them into an arrangement that best connects the pieces to the whole. She finds her design ideas in nature books, things she sees, even photos she takes. Each design is created and cut to express a message, a challenging task at times.

"I can't draw a horse's hoof," she comments. Nevertheless, she can cut art from paper, her designs running the gamut from buildings such as churches and the old Green County Courthouse to animals such as birds, goats, and sheep to religious, Victorian, Civil War, and Wilhelm Tell themes. She's even told the story of coming to America in a rendering of that name.

Schiesser's cuttings have been exhibited in Switzerland and at New York City's Museum of American Folk Art. Two of her cuttings are part of the permanent collection at the Wisconsin Folk Museum in Mount Horeb. Having first exhibited her work in 1985 at the Wilhelm Tell Art Fair in New Glarus, Elda has continued to show it at the Heidi Fest, regional art and craft fairs, the Kenosha Public Museum, and the Wisconsin Regional Artists Association. She could, if she wanted, exhibit every weekend. "I try to keep my art a hobby," she states. "I don't want it to become a job."

Increasingly she works on commissioned pieces. She has, for example, created paper cuttings for the First National Bank and Trust of New Glarus and the National Brown Swiss Association.

Schiesser tried once to teach some women about the art of paper cutting, but found they wouldn't listen. "They started unfolding and cutting before I told them. You've got to do things in the right steps, but they were too anxious to see the final result, to unfold it and see how it looked. The secret is to move the paper, not the scissors."

Elda may do one large cutting a year, first drawing it out on paper, then as she puts it, "letting the scissors tell a story."

A big project can take up to 16 hours just to cut out. No two of her cuttings are ever alike, because she never feels the same when she's creating them. And she doesn't make prints of them as is often done in Europe.

"It's original, affordable art," attests Hans Lenzlinger.

"I enjoy doing it. It's peaceful," explains Elda. Just how peaceful she found out when her husband and later her daughter suffered heart attacks.

"We knew you were there," her daughter told her later, "because we could hear you snipping away quietly . . . snip, snip, snip."

A member of the Guild of American Papercutters, Wisconsin Alliance of Artists, and Wisconsin Regional Artist Association, Elda never studied art beyond secondary school. She displays her art in her home where interested persons are welcome to view her Alpine paper cuttings. For those who can't make it personally to New Glarus to see her work, she has an illustrated flyer she sends out.

From New Glarus, trace the meanderings of the Sugar River through farm fields and woodland by biking or snowmobiling the 23-mile Sugar River State Trail. The trail, with only a 1 percent grade, even boasts a covered bridge near Brodhead, the halfway point for early Native Americans when they traveled between Lake Michigan and the Mississippi River.

Camp in the New Glarus Woods State Park and hike or bike into town. Hike or ski the Ice Age Trail, or hitch a ride on a hay wagon at the Swiss Valley Orchard, featuring European apple varieties and an apple bakery.

New Glarus has been called "the most picturesque small town in Wisconsin" and was recently voted "the town most resembling a Norman Rockwell painting" by the readers of *Wisconsin Trails* magazine. No wonder visitors from Switzerland are often heard to say, "I feel at home here."

Places to See, Eat, and Stay

New Glarus Chamber of Commerce: (608) 527-2095; (800) 527-6838.

New Glarus Bakery & Tea Room: (608) 527-2916.

Ruef's Meat Market: (608) 527-2554.

Prima Käse (cheese): (608) 938-4227.

New Glarus Brewing Co.: (608) 527-5850.

4
LAKE GENEVA
AND DELAVAN

PLAYBOY BUNNIES AND
THE CIRCUS CAPITAL

"We were country bumpkins," states Sandy Farwell, a former Playboy bunny at Hugh Hefner's last and most extravagant Playboy Club in Lake Geneva, known as the "Newport of the Midwest." Wealthy Chicagoans have summered in Lake Geneva since the 1860s, with many living here after the Great Chicago Fire of 1871 while their city properties were being rebuilt. President Calvin Coolidge once even made Lake Geneva the summer White House. But Hefner's Playboy Club made the town known round the world.

"Lake Geneva residents weren't real thrilled when they heard a Playboy Club was coming," says Farwell. "It started out that it was going to be a den of iniquity, but after awhile, it looked like fun. All Lake Geneva got to love it and would come out with their kids. This club was very family-oriented, which was not true of clubs in the cities."

Farwell, who worked at the former resort from 1968 until 1982, personally waited on Hugh Hefner and his guests a few times. Now, as a concierge for the Grand Geneva Resort and Spa, the Playboy Club's replacement, she happily reminisces with guests about those bygone days when Sammy Davis, Jr., Sonny and Cher, Liza Minnelli, Peggy Lee, and others performed here. "I have total déjà vu when I walk in the theater now. It hasn't changed that much."

"We literally crammed people into the service areas," explains Farwell, as she leads tours. "We had to sneak food because we didn't get a break in our eight hours. We'd go back in the service area to eat and the maitre d' had turned a tray stand upside down and thrown a tablecloth on it to seat another couple. There they were, so how could I eat?

"The training concept was very stylized. Back then, when you were wearing a bathing suit–type outfit, you had to be very ladylike when you bent over. It seems kind of silly now, but you went to the table, you turned your back on the people and, doing the 'bunny dip,' served them."

As a bunny for 14 years, Farwell may well have set the all-time record, the average stay usually being only three months. She was also unique in that she was married the entire time she worked as a bunny, having applied for the job as a joke when her husband told her she was as attractive as the girls at the club.

The Bunny Hutch, where the Playboy bunnies used to stay, can still be seen on the 2nd hole of the Brute golf course. Today's Grand Geneva, like the Playboy resort before it, boasts 1,300 rolling acres, Prairie School architecture, and two 18-hole PGA Championship golf courses.

Dave W. Hallenbeck was the director of golf on the property when the posh Playboy resort was named one of the top golf resorts in the United States. "The Marcus Corporation has saved a true jewel in the Midwest. Not only have they saved it but with the $20 million renovation, they have made the resort even better now than it was at Playboy's peak," states Hallenbeck. The Highlands, the former Briar Patch course designed by Pete Dye and Jack Nicklaus, retains its Scottish links character in its recent redesign by Bob Cupp. "The Brute, an American-style tour-level course with multi-tees, is such a great course," comments Hallenbeck, "because you could take seven or eight of the Brute's holes and call them signature holes. I consider No. 17 on the Brute the signature hole strictly because of the beauty." Originally carved out of farmland, the Brute has matured over the years with every hole now having a solid tree line. Accolades for the resort courses include *Golf Magazine*'s Silver Medal Award and inclusion on *Condé Nast Traveler*'s 1997 "50 Best Golf Resorts" list and "1997 Gold List."

The Grand Geneva's executive chef Robert A. Fedorko, who has worked with Paul Bocuse and Roger Verge, creates Italian cuisine that is simple, light, and fresh. "We peel, we seed, we chop the tomatoes ourselves. Italian food is very simple to give good flavor," states Fedorko. Of the food served at Ristoranté Brissago, he adds, "This is not complex cooking like your grandmother makes."

Enjoy the grand life at the Grand Geneva and throughout the Lake Geneva area with golf, fine dining, tennis, racquetball, a massage, and facials at the fitness spa. In winter, plan on cross-country and downhill skiing, snowshoeing, or horseback riding—even a full day at the spa. Though it's not possible to canoe into the Grand Geneva as Playboy guests once did, it is still possible to fly into the resort's airport, just as when the Playboy era was in full swing.

Lake Geneva offers boating, sailing, swimming, and waterskiing, plus a 21-mile shoreline hiking path. It follows an early Potawatomi trail that never runs more than about three feet from the water's edge. Learn about the rich and famous of another era on any of several seasonal boat cruises providing water views of the elegant mansions built by the Wrigley family, Montgomery Ward Thorne, Marshall Field, Borden, Maytag, and Swift. Or walk eight miles along the shoreline, viewing Victorian homes and landscaped gardens up close, then catch the boat at Williams Bay to cruise back to the Riviera Docks in Lake Geneva.

Years ago, as the stories go, wealthy families arriving by rail from Chicago would arrange to have their steam yachts waiting so they could jump off the train, board their yachts, and race across the lake. For a comparable thrill today, ride the U.S. mailboat, the *Walworth II*, which operates mid-June to mid-September. "Special delivery" here is routine. Every day mail carriers jump from the side of a moving boat, sprint up residents' piers to deposit the mail, then dash back to catch the boat. The tradition of lakeside delivery of groceries and other necessities first started back in the 1870s. Then, as now, it was far easier for the property owner or the hired help to walk about 100 yards to the pier than a half-mile or so to the nearest public road.

Between mailbox hops, the jumpers narrate the tour as it circles the 5,262-acre lake. They tell about Younglands, for example, an estate that is now luxury condominiums, but once boasted doorknobs of 14-karat gold, with both a miniature golf course and gymnasium in its attic. Watch for the Victorian boathouses which originally held steam-powered yachts, back when gasoline engines were considered too dangerous for boats. In the 1930s, summer residents came to Big Band dances at the Riviera Concourse, now the restored pavilion bustling with shops and busy excursion boat docks.

Even today Lake Geneva is still very much a playground for the elite. When the lakefront property of a private military academy came on the market in 1995, the acre lots ranged in price from $199,000 to $990,000. There's no other lake or area that commands such a price, according to the developer.

Before Lake Geneva was a Chicago resort community, its gristmills and sawmills drew farmers from as far away as Milwaukee, Kenosha, and Beloit for the economical milling from a 14-foot waterfall drop. And in pre–Civil War days, slaves passed through this town en route to the Great Lakes ports and freedom in Canada. For a taste of Lake Geneva's rural heritage, pick your own strawberries and raspberries at Valley View Farm, not far from where Wisconsin's first 4-H Club was organized in 1914.

Use the pamphlet "A Walking Tour of Olde Lake Geneva Towne" (available at the Chamber of Commerce) to discover the site of the 1880 Odell Typewriter Factory and of the Lake House, the area's earliest hotel circa 1837, which was destroyed by fire in the late 1920s. The Ice King, John Vose Seymour, lived in the Gurdon Montague House at 1134 Geneva Street around 1855. He 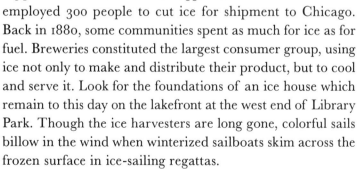 employed 300 people to cut ice for shipment to Chicago. Back in 1880, some communities spent as much for ice as for fuel. Breweries constituted the largest consumer group, using ice not only to make and distribute their product, but to cool and serve it. Look for the foundations of an ice house which remain to this day on the lakefront at the west end of Library Park. Though the ice harvesters are long gone, colorful sails billow in the wind when winterized sailboats skim across the frozen surface in ice-sailing regattas.

Any time of year, learn all about the stars at the University of Chicago's Yerkes Observatory, on Lake Geneva's shore in Williams Bay (Saturday tours only). A 40-inch lens, the world's largest refracting telescope, sits beneath the movable dome of this 1897 building.

Just down the road is Delavan, the birthplace of P. T. Barnum's "Greatest Show on Earth" and the "19th-century Circus Capital of the Nation." In 1847, a year before Wisconsin attained statehood and 37 years before the Ringling Brothers raised their first canvas in Baraboo, the Mabie brothers chose Delavan as the winter quarters for their U.S. Olympic Circus, the largest traveling show in America at the time. For almost 50 years, between 1847 and 1894, no fewer than 26 circuses spent their winter here.

Why was Delavan chosen as a winter home base? Primarily because of the horses. In the 19th-century circus, the horse was its most important asset, both for transportation and performing. Delavan had abundant pasture land, plenty of pure water in lakes and streams, and a four-season climate, all important for the well-being of draft and performing horses. At the same time, the nation was expanding to the west, so most circuses were leaving their eastern quarters to relocate in the new, bustling territories in the upper Mississippi Valley.

The Mabie Circus, which quartered at the site of Lake Lawn Lodge on Delavan Lake, launched a Wisconsin circus dynasty. Over 115 shows were organized in the state over the next hundred years. In the center of town, look for the statue of the elephant Romeo. Though a star attraction of the Mabie Circus, he had a reprehensible reputation, having killed five trainers in 10 years. Use your imagination to turn back the clock, visualizing elephants on Walworth Avenue, zebras grazing on north 7th Street, and equestrians and acrobats practicing in area barns.

Back in 1868, when the circus came to town, a 13-year-old Delavan resident, Edward Tilden, could not afford the 15-cent admission price. He vowed that someday he would make a lot of money and bring the circus to town with free admission for all. Three years later, he dropped out of school and walked to Chicago with 14 cents in his pocket. Over time, he amassed a fortune in meat packing and banking interests and remembered his youthful vow. In 1912, 1913, and 1914, he put on a free picnic-circus for every child in Walworth County, even providing free transportation from each city. The free shows were held at his Delavan Lake property, present site of Lake Lawn Lodge. Tilden had every intention of continuing the free circus annually, but death intervened. When his funeral train arrived in Delavan from Chicago, over 2,600 people, mostly children, were waiting at the depot in sub-zero February weather to pay their respects.

Delavan's circus era came to an end in 1894, the circus-ring barns and landmarks all disappearing within a generation. But many outstanding early circus stars are still here, buried in Delavan's Spring Grove and St. Andrew's cemeteries. The local chamber of commerce has a guide to the sites, plus a walking tour of historic downtown. Look for the more than 130 graves of animal trainers, equestrians, trapeze artists, wardrobe workers, clowns, show owners, and musicians, each identified with a special circus marker and number. Winter or summer, it makes a great walk.

Before departing town, be sure to see and maybe even book an overnight stay at the 1885 Allyn Mansion Inn. This elegant 23-room B&B, at 511 E. Walworth Avenue, boasts three parlors, parquet floors, and 10 marble and onyx fireplaces. Lovingly restored over a period of years, this National Register property won the 1992 Grand Prize in the National Trust's Great American Home Awards.

Delavan invites other discoveries as well. Learn how 1800s-era utilitarian reproductions are handcrafted and salt-glazed at Shadowlawn Pottery, at 5904 Mound Road. Cut your own Christmas tree, or buy it precut directly from the grower, from Thanksgiving to December 24, at Ron Piening's Harmas Farms.

But most of all, always remember Delavan for its circus heritage. Paraphrasing Pablo Picasso, "Circuses make us laugh. . . . Circuses are for the young and old. . . . It takes a long time to become young."

Places to See, Eat, and Stay

Lake Geneva Area Chamber of Commerce: (414) 248-4416; (800) 345-1020.

Grand Geneva Resort and Spa: (414) 248-8811; (800) 558-3417.

Delavan/Delavan Lake Chamber of Commerce: (414) 728-5095; (800) 624-0052.

Geneva Lake Cruise Line: (414) 248-6206; (800) 558-5911.

Allyn Mansion Inn: (414) 728-9090.

5

ELKHART LAKE

ROAD RACING AND
CHOCOLATE SODAS

"Coming from turn 4 into turn 5, they're probably going 175 to 180 MPH; decelerating to go around the curve at about 75, maybe 85 MPH, then back up the hill, up to throttle; under the Corvette Bridge, then a real sharp 90-degree left. How do they do it? I don't know. I can do it at about 65 MPH," confides Roger Jaynes, director of public relations for Road America. Road America's four-mile, 14-turn track, the racing home of Wisconsin's most thrilling Indy and formula car races, ranks with the very best road-racing circuits in the world. It has tested the driving skills of some of the best drivers and automobiles: A. J. Foyt; Bruce McLaren; Al Unser, Jr.; Carroll Shelby; Jim Hall; Phil Hill; Rick Mears; Swede Savage; Roger Penske; and more.

"They go through the Carousel, which is like a giant merry-go-round, at about 125 to 130 MPH, almost full speed," Jaynes continues. "The drivers like Road America because it has three straightaways, wide sweeping turns, hairpin turns, and lots of places you can pass. The largest road course in North America, it compares to Formula One courses in Europe.

"As Mario Andretti always says, 'You can show off your driving ability here because there are places to pass, dice with people, make moves, and really race.' Andretti rates Road America one of the top five tracks in the world, calling it a beautiful track in a beautiful setting."

According to Jaynes, "The street courses in the middle of a city are so tight, there are usually only one or two places where drivers can really pass, which makes for boring racing. All along the course at Road America there are places to pass, and that's what the fans like to see—wheel-to-wheel racing.

"Before Road America, sports cars officially raced through the streets of Elkhart Lake and out into the countryside on a 10-mile course," explains Jaynes. "After World War II, guys who were in the service in Europe who had seen what a Maserati or Ferrari, Triumph, and MG looked like, were taken with them and ordered them. They became a fad.

"Street racing effectively ended when the state of Wisconsin ruled that public streets could not be used for private purposes. But Clif Tufte and some businessmen, many of whom were members of the Chicago Region Sports Car Club of America (SCCA), wanted to see the racing continued. Tufte, who had been looking around for a place to build a track, found two farms with a total of 525 acres. At a luncheon in Chicago in 1954, the businessmen decided to go forward with the project. Road America was incorporated with Tufte as the first president."

Tufte, a civil engineer, would go out for Sunday drives, and if he came to a turn he liked, he measured it and included it in the course. He felt that the whole idea was to have a racecourse that could be driven, one that the drivers would find challenging.

"Because this is Kettle Moraine countryside, there were huge glacial boulders that had to be dug out and moved.

Where the present Carousel runs, a huge hill had to be cut in half. The track was completed and asphalted, with the pagoda and scoring tower still being built the week of the first race. But everything was completed so the races could run on September 10 and 11, 1955. The main race turned out to be probably one of the greatest races in the history of the track. Phil Hill, who would go on to be the first Grand Prix champion from the United States, edged out Sherwood Johnston by about four inches.

After that, the event just grew. A June sports-car event, Trans Am pro racing, and Indy cars were added, as were motorcycles in the 1980s, and, most recently, off-road vehicles (motocross).

"We now have probably the widest lineup of quality racing of any track in the United States, plus the largest vintage weekend with over $50 million in classic and antique race cars," says Jaynes. "The Indy weekend is our most popular because that is the premier series in the United States and all the stars are here—Bobby Rahal, Danny Sullivan, Mario and Michael Andretti.

"This is a major league facility, not only the largest road course in North America, but a state-of-the-art facility. In addition to nine suites which companies rent on race weekends, every one of the 35 pits is individually wired with pods for electricity, computer, TV, water, you name it. The Indy cars are so sophisticated now that Emerson Fittipaldi will go out and do three or four laps at speed, come in, download the car's computer into his laptop and sit there and have a 3-D full-color image of the track. It will tell him that when he was going into turn 5 he lost about a second and a half. At Indy, they don't have the pods in the pit area, but they have them back in the garages. In many ways, our facility is actually superior to Indianapolis in terms of what's right here and available for the drivers."

Food at Road America has been voted the best on the Indy car circuit by writers who cover racing. "The favorite for years and years has been the hot ears of sweet corn with butter, bratwurst, and beer," enthuses Jaynes.

Twelve concession stands sponsored by local organizations offer a wide variety of excellent food for extremely reasonable prices. Volunteers from St. John the Baptist Church provide German potato salad, sandwiches, and pies. Across from Corvette Corral at the Rotary Roundup Cafe, you'll find Miesfeld's award-winning brats and Miesfeld's brat-on-a-stick. Munchwerkes, with three locations around the track, offers brats, cheeseburgers, corn on the cob, and the egger (a 12-item omelette). Its No. 9 location serves the latter with blueberry muffins and hash browns.

Other concession stands and Road America's own gift shop sell over 1,100 racing mementos, from pins, patches, model cars, and automotive artwork to clothing items such as ties, caps, sweatshirts, and jackets. The proverbial T-shirts are here too. One reads, "With 488 cubic inches under the hood, it doesn't need a prancing horse on the grill." Another by SWB Studios quotes Mark Donohue: "If you can make black marks on a straight from the time you turn out of a corner until the braking point of the next turn, then you have enough horse power."

Road America, according to Jaynes, tries to provide a family atmosphere, with kids under 12 admitted free. "We want parents to bring their children along, come up here, spend a couple of days, be out in the sunshine, and really enjoy the racing. It's like being on a picnic with race cars going by at the same time."

The 525 acres give plenty of green space for spreading out and moving from location to location during a race. During race weekends, the paddock areas are packed with motor homes for competitors and tents for the cars and crews. A good viewing area is turn 5, where corporate tents are set up and people can get right up against the fence. Often the bluff on the hill by turn 7 is filled with spectators too.

Jaynes says, the Road America crowd really likes to move around. "They'll have two or three places that they really like to view from. They'll watch at turn 5 for awhile, then maybe come up to the paddock area and sit, or go down by turn 1, then come back to the main straight grandstand. They like to meander. They really don't like to stay in one place."

People with motor homes tend to make a weekend of it. Though it's not possible to camp overnight at Road America, a lot of people drive in with their motor homes. One of the favorite places for this crowd to congregate is the turn 3 area, with parking near the track. While the kids play Frisbee, moms and dads sit in their folding chairs watching the races. Others bring bicycles, pedaling along the access road from one viewpoint to another, stopping for a snack now and then.

And, just how did Canada Corner get its name? In the early years of the track, back in the late fifties and early sixties, people drove their own personal sports cars to Road America and raced them. A Canadian fellow "lost it in the turn, punching his car up real bad," recounts Jaynes. "After the race was over, Clif met the guy in the paddock area and learned that he didn't have a car to drive home. Clif gave him some money for transportation and said, 'From here on, I'm going to name that turn after you. It's going to be Canada Corner.'" When people came from Canada after that, they'd sit at turn 12.

Though Road America draws more than 200,000 people in a season for its six big summer weekends, those event are only part of what Road America is all about. From mid-April to the first of October, the track is in use every day, with perhaps only a dozen days total set aside for maintenance. Sign up for a chance to drive the course with one of the many car clubs that rent Road America's track for their own use, including nonspectator and vintage races.

In addition to the private and corporate groups using Road America, Skip Barber's Racing School operates here as well. Grand Prix hopefuls trade in their sedans for something a little sportier, the most popular course being the three-day racing school. After instruction in safety techniques, the classroom moves to the track, where students experience high-speed thrills while learning how to maneuver, downshift, brake, corner, and double-clutch Formula Dodge racing cars. Barber's school, 20 years old in 1995, trained close to one-third of the starting drivers for the Indianapolis 500 from 1985 to 1995. But the school is not just for aspiring pros. Thousands graduate every year, ranging from rookies beginning professional racing careers, to homemakers and high school students, to sports stars and senior citizens.

During Road America's annual vintage weekend, individuals need not just stand behind the fence and watch. Some actually race their restored $250,000 Cobras, Can-Ams, and Ferraris, pitting their driving skills against the likes of Bob Bondurant or Brian Redman as they go screaming down the straightaways or side-by-side through the kink.

During this nostalgic weekend, a Concours d'Elegance traditionally takes place on East and Lake Streets in downtown Elkhart Lake early on Friday and Saturday evenings. Grandparents leaning on canes, svelte young women in evening attire, and moms and dads in shorts with babes in arms come to view and admire the magnificent array of vintage and historic automobiles. The night begins with the entire collection of 50 or more cars roaring into town. Spectators lining the streets thrill to the sound called *power*.

Later, once the cars are parked on display, the crowd mingles, sipping beer and wine, chatting with owners, renewing acquaintances. Conversations revolve around $100,000 engines, past races, the millions of dollars of inventory displayed, and Elkhart Lake as it used to be.

"I saw this car race at Meadowdale (Illinois) at the first race I ever attended."

"Have you got yours picked out yet?" someone asks a companion, as they slowly wander in and out through the maze of gleaming Jaguars, Porsches, Corvettes, and Ferraris.

"That's the kind of car they used to race on the streets here," a beaming father proudly tells his young son.

Located in the heart of scenic Kettle Moraine State Forest, Elkhart Lake quickly became a resort community in the late 19th century. The natural spring-fed lake, which resembles the shape of an elk's heart, was named by the Native Americans who used its pure waters as a spa. The area, settled by German immigrants, catered to the Chicago trade arriving by train. The Depot Museum chronicling the community's history is housed in the 100-year-old railroad station, located at the corner of Rhine and Lake Streets. It's open June 1 to Labor Day.

At first, friends and relatives visited residents of the community, staying in their big old homes. They liked the area so much, they would ask if they could bring friends on the next trip, or if someone had a room to rent so they could stay a week or more. Eventually, trains brought whole families, the mothers and children staying for several weeks during the summer, with fathers commuting back to Chicago to work during the week.

With the influx of visitors, seven resorts sprang up around the lake. Today's Barefoot Bay Resort was once known as the Lake View House. The nearby Osthoff Condominium Resort, opened in 1995, sits on the original site of the 1885 Osthoff Hotel.

Siebkens Resort, founded in 1916, continues its Old World traditions of gracious hospitality and fine food. Ollie Siebkens, the resort's original owner, was the first local woman to get a loan from a bank. She ran the resort all alone, a job it takes four of her heirs to do now.

Back in 1917, rooms rented for $3.25 a day and $20 a week. You won't be able to stay today for that kind of money, but a night's sleep in Paul Newman's room will cost under $100. Yes, Paul Newman did sleep in Room 11 at this Victorian inn while filming the movie *Winning*. He came, too, as a race driver for Indy races at Road America. If you're planning a stay, keep in mind that vintage and Indy weekends fill up six months ahead, and weekends are always busy May through September.

Siebkens has been featured on ESPN as one of the greatest stops for racers on the Indy car tour. In the resort's main building, photos of famous racers line the walls of a small paddock-style bar off the dining room. Siebkens Tavern serves racing crews from around the world during summer racing season and lucky visitors may find themselves rubbing shoulders with international race stars. Look for the tavern in the basement of a former opera house, now converted into an antiques shop. Carrying through the vintage decor, tables rest on old sewing machine treadles. There's a large screened-in porch; a beer garden at the tavern's north end; and a tiny, intimate porch, just big enough for one table, at the south end.

Yvonne Gessert Landgraf, an Elkhart Lake village trustee, had grandparents who worked at the old Osthoff, her grandmother as a waitress and her grandfather as a handyman who also helped with the pigeon loft the hotel had for homing pigeons. Her parents opened a store and confectionery in 1922 where they also sold tickets for the interurban rail line. Landgraf and her husband Ed have continued to run Gessert's on Lake Street each summer (open daily, Memorial Day to Labor Day), since her parents retired in 1978.

In the old days, everyone in the family helped with the business. Yvonne's grandfather was a rural letter carrier in the area. With population sparse at that time, he often finished his route in half a day, freeing him to deliver ice cream around the lake in the afternoon. Yvonne remembers that ladies planning a bridge party would often call in and order two pints of Neapolitan or three pints of chocolate and vanilla. The pints were packed in pails with shaved ice and salt. In those good old days when ice cream was about 25 or 35 cents a pint, there was no additional charge for delivery.

Gessert's continues to serve up old-fashioned ice cream parlor treats like sodas, phosphates, and flavored cokes. "We're especially known for our chocolate ice cream sodas and our phosphates," says Landgraf. "Every year people come special from St. Louis. Here for race weekend, they drop by three different times for our chocolate sodas before they fly home."

In addition to traditional sundaes with strawberry or hot fudge sauce, Gessert's serves up its very own special concoctions including Golden Glow—butter pecan ice cream capped with maple syrup and pecan bits—and Dinosaur Freckles—M&Ms over dinosaur green (mint) ice cream, topped with hot fudge. There's even a mint shake, a grasshopper without the alcohol.

Gessert's still has the pressed tin ceiling, terrazzo floor, old-fashioned booths, and antique display showcases, now used to show off specialty candy and gift items. Landgraf remembers that the interurban train delivering the showcases became stuck in a snowstorm near Crystal Lake, so they were taken off the train and transferred to Elkhart Lake by bobsled.

With all the rooming houses in town, restaurants were needed. Hundreds of eggs were served on July weekends, as were plate lunches and dinners of steaks and fries. Following evening activities at the resorts, young people flocked to

Gessert's for late-night sandwiches and malteds. The crowds were so large in the 1940s, in fact, that Yvonne's parents opened a second fountain.

Many marriages were made in Elkhart Lake, which became a kind of mecca for the singles set in the 1950s. Landgraf's mother ran a rooming house with the help of a housekeeper. Every room had a sink, with several young women staying in the same room. Though the rooms were designed to house four, the young ladies would often arrive with a couple of friends in tow, saying, "We've brought two more, Mrs. Gessert, hope you don't mind. We'll sleep cross-wise on the beds." Those days were not as informal as the nineties, Yvonne states. "Each girl had numerous suitcases and changed clothes maybe six times a day."

Elkhart Lake, always popular with those of German descent, in 1888 became the setting for a 600-acre estate, complete with a $200,000 villa modeled after a Rhine castle.

Elkhart Lake's year-round population consistently hovers around 1,000. There used to be more hustle and bustle in town when the office for Road America was located in what is now Nordic Accents, adjacent to Gessert's. "Then," Landgraf says, "MGs and other sports cars would go snorting around Elkhart Lake, as race fans stopped by to pick up tickets and passes."

In addition to the modernized resorts on the lake and B&Bs in Victorian or log homes, there's plenty of camping nearby. Walk the pedestrian mall in front of the new Osthoff complex to reach the public park and beach, a great viewing area for the sailboat races on summer Sundays. Or hike the five-mile Potawatomi Indian Trail circling the lake.

Tour a broom factory and Rolling Meadows Sorghum Mill by appointment. Camp, hunt, and fish at the Broughton-Sheboygan Marsh Park or use it as an access point for 175 miles of county snowmobile trails.

Both the marsh and nearby northern unit of the Kettle Moraine State Forest make superb locations for wildlife viewing any time of year. Hike and cross-country ski the Ice Age National Scenic Trail, visiting the Henry Reuss Ice Age Visitor Center for maps and schedules of naturalist programs. For a display of Native American artifacts and tools at an archaeological dig site and no-license trout fishing, look for Henschel's Indian Museum and Hidden Springs Trout Farm three miles out of town (open Tuesday through Saturday, Memorial Day to Labor Day; other times by appointment).

Gary Knowles, who grew up in Elkhart Lake, remembers back to the days when it was considered exotic to have a foreign car, even a Triumph made in England. A lifelong car enthusiast, he has joined forces with Alex McDonell, a former race-car driver, to form a global organization, the International Classic Auto Tours, Ltd. (ICAT; P.O. Box 44082; Madison, WI 53711). Knowles, McDonell, and their car-loving members believe that the finest automobile is one that's in motion, roads unwinding as ribbons of beauty and history, playgrounds where drivers enjoy the pinnacle of the driving experience. In past years Knowles and McDonell have organized major annual gatherings for auto enthusiasts, including the Sports Car and GT Classic, a fall Wisconsin wild goose chase, and the Wisconsin Convertible Classic.

The annual convertible tour marks the anniversary of what may well have been the world's first auto race. In 1873, an outbreak of equine distemper sent most of Wisconsin's horses to the sick bay for weeks. In that same year the Spark—a light, self-propelled highway vehicle—was built by Dr. Carhart of Racine. Recognizing the value of this new alternative to keep the wheels of commerce and agriculture turning, the Wisconsin Legislature, in 1875, offered a prize of $10,000 to the state citizen who could produce a machine "which shall be a cheap and practical substitute for the use of horses and other animals on the highway and farm." Such a machine was to perform a journey of at least 200 miles, "propelled by its own internal power, at the average rate of at least five miles per hour, working time." By July 1878, two steam-powered vehicles were ready to run the prescribed course from Green Bay to Madison.

Knowles, referring to the State of Wisconsin Historical Society Records and talks with family descendants, tells the rest of the story like this: "The big purse led to the development of six vehicles and on July 17, 1878, two of them steamed to the starting line. The Oshkosh and the Green Bay raced through the Fox Cities toward Madison, stirring up clouds of dust, parading before cheering crowds, and startling livestock along the way. Mechanical failure plagued the Green Bay and only the Oshkosh reached Madison. It took just 33 hours and 27 minutes for the winner to cover the distance—an average speed of approximately six MPH. Alexander Gallinger, builder of the Oshkosh, claimed the prize. But the legislature, like all true fans, wanted 'tougher and faster.' They gave him $5,000 and said they expected better. Gallinger told them to keep the money and steamed back home."

Places to See, Eat, and Stay

Road America: (920) 892-4576; (800) 365-RACE.

Elkhart Lake Chamber of Commerce: (920) 876-2922.

Siebkens Resort: (920) 876-2600; (888) 876-2600.

Henry Reuss Ice Age Visitor Center: (920) 533-8322.

Rolling Meadows Sorghum Mill: (920) 876-2182.

Henshel's Indian Museum and Hidden Springs Trout Farm: (920) 876-3193.

6
KOHLER
PAMPERED BY PLUMBING

Back in 1883, John Michael Kohler enameled the rim and inside surfaces of a combination cattle watering trough and hog scalder, added feet, and sold it as a bathtub. The rest is history, as the saying goes.

Kohler village, described as "a garden at industry's gate," sits adjacent to Kohler Co., the nation's leading manufacturer of plumbing products. So appealing is this small planned community, one hour north of Milwaukee, that it was recently chosen as the location to build and showcase "The Most Romantic Home in America."

"Kohler Co. and Kohler village are concrete examples of true entrepreneurship in action," said John Lillesand, senior vice president of technical services for Kohler Co. in a 1990 speech to the Friends of the State Historical Society. "They are real-life examples of the daring, the risk-taking, the foresight, the creative spirit it takes to be a success. Not an overnight, get-rich-quick and run-with-the-money success, but rather the success that endures, that endows, that benefits the multitudes, that imbues the spirits of people to take what is good and amplify it into even greater success."

Founder Kohler envisioned more than a successful factory and foundry. Though he
didn't live to see his dream become a
reality, he dreamed of building a model
city and passed that dream on to his
family. When Sheboygan become too
congested, he built a new factory in
Riverside, later renamed Kohler.

Walter, Kohler's son, took up the vision, defining the philosophy this way: "What a man earns and how he earns it are
always important to him. But it is equally important that he
live in a community where there is a chance to be happy and
comfortable, acquire a home of his own, and enjoy the things
that make life worth living. He must make a living, of course,
but he ought to have a chance to enjoy living."

Visits to European industrial garden cities of the early
1900s influenced the development of Kohler village. Distinct
zones were established for industry, business, farming, and
residences. Broad, curving streets conformed to the topography, and land was set aside for parks and playgrounds
throughout. A green belt, still in existence today, circled the
plant and village, serving not only to define the village and
prevent future encroachment, but also to keep the smoke from
stacks in times gone by from reaching the populated areas.

In his 1990 speech, John Lillesand continued with more
history of the company village: "The one difference from
European communities was that here the town would not be
company owned. Rather, employees would purchase their
own home in the American tradition. Kohler purchased land
adjacent to his factory, deeding it to a home improvement
company which then built homes and sold them at cost."
Kohler also purchased outlying farms with the aim of preserving the nearby river, preventing land speculation, and
providing orderly growth.

Initial plans for Kohler, according to Lillesand, included the first subdivision, West I, and the placement of many of today's village landmarks such as the American Club (a luxury inn), the school, Ravine Park, and stores in the building where the Design Center is now located. Other features, including horse fountains, an ice plant, livery stable, and blacksmith shop, were peculiar to the times.

Look for the early residences, patterned after English cottages in combinations of wood, brick, stucco, and stone, as you drive down School Street, just south of the American Club. A second residential area of brick homes and cottages, started in 1924, sits south of the factory. The "Most Romantic House," a recent joint project of Kohler Co. and *Traditional Home* magazine, has been sold and is no longer available for tours, though plans for the 3,200-square-foot showcase house are available through the magazine.

The Olmsted Brothers firm in Massachusetts, known for its designs of New York City's Central Park and the Harvard University campus, planned the third residential area, West II, just west of the original development. Here, along curving streets bisected by interurban and railroad lines, buyers could choose from a variety of designs: English, American, Colonial, and traditional bungalow.

Because the social and cultural development of the village's residents was as important as the physical development of the village, the Kohler Recreation Club was organized. There were bowling, basketball, and baseball leagues; clubs for tennis, skating, and pistol and rifle marksmanship; and a band and chorus.

Women played a key role in the life and improvement of the community through the Kohler Woman's Club, organized by Marie Kohler, daughter of the company's founder. For 34 years the club held a Better Homes week, part of a national movement promoting demonstration homes with the newest in modern living. The Distinguished Guest series, another legacy of the Woman's Club, according to Lillesand, "brought to the village famous artists, statesmen, and entertainers including Admiral Richard Byrd, Dr. Norman Vincent Peale, Pearl Buck, Mary Martin, Burl Ives, and the Trapp Family Singers."

In 1977, the Frank Lloyd Wright Foundation was contracted to develop a modernized 50-year master plan for the more than 4,500 acres within the village limits. In the residential areas, the new Wright guidelines provide for greater diversity of design than earlier plans.

River Wildlife, the first project of the Wright plan, comprised a 500-acre wildlife preserve set aside for future generations. This private membership club—American Club guests can get day passes—is used for hiking and horseback riding, cross-country skiing in winter, hunting and clay shooting, and dining on "country gourmet" cuisine in a secluded rustic log lodge.

Development of The Sports Core, a complete health, racquet, and physical fitness facility, followed the wildlife project. Then came the renovation of the American Club, a historic building remodeled into a luxurious inn, the Midwest's only AAA five-diamond resort hotel.

The Pete Dye–designed Blackwolf Run golf course was "the next jewel in hospitality's crown," according to Lillesand, preserving a part of the meandering Sheboygan River from unsightly development. Rated one of the top four public golf courses in the nation, Blackwolf Run is "target golf" at its finest, with pot bunkers, severe mounding, and natural rough areas. Dye's trademarks—railroad tie bunkers, desert-size sandtraps, and rolling mounds of prairie grass—make up part of the 400-acre picturesque and challenging setting.

Golf aficionados know Blackwolf Run as the scene of the 1995 U.S. Regional Semifinals and U.S. Regional Championship of the Andersen Consulting World Championship of Golf, and of the 1998 U.S. Women's Open Championship. Though anybody can play the course, the biggest problem is booking availability. Guests at the American Club hotels book tee times when making a room reservation, ensuring they'll get on the course during their vacation.

Kohler's new Whistling Straits links-style layout, also designed by Pete Dye, has 14 holes within a stone's throw of the Lake Michigan shoreline. True to the original traditions of golf, it was planned as a walking course. As he planned the 8th green—unobstructed earth, water, and sky with an unrecoverable penalty for miscalculation—Dye was heard to remark: "I can hear 'em cursing me already. They'll love me and hate me on every hole of this course." The Clubhouse, in the style of an Irish country farmstead, is behind the bank, giving the Straits course unobstructed shoreline views of this Great Lake.

There is no better place to appreciate the rich history of Kohler village than in the Tudor-style American Club with its gabled roof and dormer windows. This luxurious inn, listed on the National Register of Historic Places, celebrated its 75th anniversary in 1993. Today it sits amid manicured lawns and formal English gardens, but back in 1918 it was built to house immigrant workers at the Kohler Co. "A worker deserves not only wages, but roses as well," said Walter J. Kohler, Sr., president of Kohler Co. from 1905 to 1940 and governor of Wisconsin from 1929 to 1931.

"Single men of modest means" were the American Club's first guests. For men employed at the Kohler factory, it was a place to dine, sleep, and relax after working hours, while adjusting to their new country. Dutchmen, Austrians, Russians, and Germans ate together in what is now the Wisconsin Room, where two immense American flags draped the walls. Of the flags, Walter Kohler said they were there "for the purpose of ever keeping before the men the fact that they are living in America and not a foreign country."

Kohler encouraged his employees to study and learn English in order to be able to take out papers to become citizens. Evening classes was held at the nearby school two nights a week. In 1930, the company newspaper reported that 678 immigrants had taken out "first papers" since 1919. Kohler encouraged Americanization by giving banquets for the newly naturalized citizens, and full wages on the day they went to the courthouse during working hours to become citizens. He saw the American Club, and the American flag which he displayed so prominently, as being a way to positively influence generations to come and to instill a love of country to men born and reared elsewhere. Like Willa Cather, Kohler believed that "the history of every country begins in the heart of a man or a woman."

A highly awarded meeting site, the American Club has been recognized as one of America's most romantic getaways. Each guest room honors a famous American with photos and memorabilia on the walls. All bathrooms include a Kohler whirlpool bath. In fact, when the American Club served as the immigrant dormitory, the washrooms located throughout the building featured the luxury of hot running water any time of day and were noted to have the best lavatories, toilets, and bathtubs that could be found anywhere in the country.

This distinction of superior baths holds true today. Exceptional amenities in guest bathrooms include Kohler plumbing fixtures, ranging from marble-lined baths to seven-foot oval Super Bath whirlpools, and from greenhouse-enclosed spas to the Kohler multifunction MasterShower tower with four showerheads and 10 push-button electronic keypad control. A Kohler Habitat Masterbath indulges the senses with cycles of sun, steam, soft rain, and gentle breezes. Hotel rates are based not on the season or size of the room, but rather the accoutrements of the bath. Here, a tub is not just a tub!

If the dazzling array of choices overwhelms and confuses

you, check out the possibilities first at the nearby Kohler Design Center with its great wall of china, designer baths, and 15 working whirlpools. On the lower level, a museum traces the history of the company and Kohler village. It's open seven days a week, including holidays, and admission is free.

Visit, too, the factory where the vitreous china and enameled cast-iron plumbing products are made. Tours, offered on weekdays (with the exception of holidays and the annual summer shutdown) at 8:30 A.M. and lasting about three hours, are led by retired Kohler Co. employees. Wear comfortable walking shoes for this unusual industrial journey, the only spot in the United States where such a variety of processes are observed in one factory tour.

A cold winter's day makes an ideal time to visit the oftentimes sweltering and noisy shop floor. Peek into giant kilns, over 300 feet long, where wet clay toilets are baked, then watch inspectors test the finished china for cracks. Feel the heat from molten iron, glowing red hot, being poured into molds to create cast-iron sinks and tubs. For reservations, which are required, call the Design Center.

The Immigrant Room, the American Club's showcase restaurant, emphasizes Wisconsin's bounty. What used to be the bowling alley for employees has been converted into a setting both elegant and intimate. Comprising a series of six authentically decorated dining rooms, the Immigrant Room reflects the state's European heritage—the French, English, Dutch, Scandinavian, and German groups who settled the region. Diners feel as if they are visiting an undiscovered country inn and celebrating the spirit of America and Americans too.

Back in 1918, a resident of the American Club paid a monthly fee of $27.50 for a single room, board, and "plain washing." Food was hearty and plentiful. During meals, a Victrola played marches by John Philip Sousa, the "March King," who twice performed in Kohler Village. Every Fourth of July, the American Club continues to celebrate all things American with a Sousa concert, Dixieland jazz with an ice cream social, barbershop quartets, croquet, horseshoes, and pink lemonade. Bunting and flags everywhere make it a real hometown celebration in America's heartland.

A day visitor to Kohler who is not a resort guest might opt to tour the factory and/or Design Center; book a massage, herbal wrap, or facial at the Sports Core; and spend the afternoon shopping at Woodlake or touring Waelderhaus, typical of houses in the Bregenzerwald region of Austria (the Kohler family's ancestral homeland).

You can also plan a picnic in Ravine, Roosevelt, or Lost Woods Park and walk, jog, or bike on the 17-mile Old Plank Road Recreational Trail at the north end of the village. As 11 miles are paved, rollerblading is even a possibility.

Yet another option is to sign up for classes in traditional and classic cooking techniques with École de Cuisine, the only French cooking school of its kind in the Midwest. Learn the art of making vichyssoise or consommé of duck, crème brûlée, or chocolate tarts. Special events and classes, which may be taken with or without hotel accommodations at the American Club, are hosted by visiting culinary professionals, chefs from the American Club, touring cookbook authors, and founder Jill Prescott. Instruction varies from one day or a weekend to a week in length. Look for the school and its associated cookware retail store in the Shops at Woodlake Kohler.

At the end of a busy day in Kohler, drop in for a beer at the Horse & Plow, a true "world-class" pub, according to manager John Shovan. "What makes us world-class is the quality of our offerings," he explains. "For example, we have 12 Wisconsin draft beers on tap, including Black Bavarian and Special Amber from Sprecher in Milwaukee, Hefeweiss and a seasonal tap from Capital Brewing in Middleton, and

Alderbrau Porter or Stout from Appleton Brewing. These are all absolutely top-quality American beers brewed in the European style—you will never mistake them for the traditional American beer."

Not sure what to order from a list of well over 60 beers? Try the Horse & Plow beer sampling program that allows patrons a five-ounce sample of six different beers at a special price. Glasses are presented on a placemat similar to those used for wine and Scotch tastings, complete with information about each beer printed alongside each glass.

In preparation for the holidays, the American Club sponsors the Wisconsin Holiday Market, a juried ethnic arts and crafts show, with items like Ukranian-decorated eggs, antique chalkware, folk art, weavings, and ornaments. At Kohler's annual "In Celebration of Chocolate," a feast of fanciful concoctions is consumed by a chocolate-entranced crowd. "We create a fairyland of chocolate dreams for one night, and then—poof!—it's gone," comments Tom van Duursen, director of food and beverages for the event.

Preparations for the chocolate celebration begin six months in advance, when pastry chef Richard Palm and his team begin considering themes for the holiday party. Complicating their efforts is their self-imposed standing rule that a dessert may not be repeated. Thus, much of the summer is spent researching recipe books and gathering ideas for novel chocolate preparations. After testing, a final menu is confirmed listing at least 20 different types of tortes and pastries, as well as ice creams, truffles, specialty foods (including some exotic creations such as chocolate ravioli), and spectacular show pieces.

Once the gold foil–wrapped bricks of the world's finest imported and domestic chocolate—600 pounds in all—are delivered, preparations begin in earnest. Recipes are organized into an intricate schedule of preparatory steps, enabling all the dishes to be completed just in time for the grand all-chocolate buffet.

Precisely at 7 P.M. on the appointed day, the ballroom doors open to reveal a buffet stretching 100 feet, laden with tiers of chocolate delights: dozens of cakes and tortes and thousands of individual candies. In addition to gourmet chocolates from Europe and throughout the United States, there are specialties from Wisconsin chocolatiers. The cost for this chocolate ecstasy is about $35 per person, with reservations required.

All the American Club's celebrations, including one for antiques (March) and another for spring gardens (late April and early May), intertwine country elegance, hospitality, and memories of things past. Hugo Silva-Tobar, a native Chilean and now a naturalized United States citizen, summed up his visit to Kohler and the American Club by penning these words:

> Walking through the halls of the American Club and seeing the photos of the early Kohler workers at work and play . . . remind me of what brought me to this country and what the United States continues to promise to newcomers. . . . The history of the American Club and my own immigration experience combined to make me feel more at home there than like a guest.

Kohler and the American Club continue to fulfill dreams.

Places to See, Eat, and Stay

Kohler Visitor Information: (920) 458-3450.

American Club: (920) 457-8000; (800) 344-2838.

Kohler Design Center: (920) 457-3699.

École de Cuisine: (920) 451-9151.

7

WASHINGTON ISLAND

LOOMS AND A STAVKIRKE

"What I love about this place is that you have the amenities of a town, but what you really have is country. If you have three cars at a corner, you think you have a traffic jam. People say, 'Where's the town?' and I tell them, I think you passed through it!'" says Washington Island resident Marilyn Domer.

"The island flies on its own. We have our own activities and are very self-sufficient. We as an island offer more than any one township in Door County, where the towns and villages rely on each other. Volunteerism runs rampant," says Bonnie Munao, past president of the Washington Island Chamber of Commerce.

"People who move here have generally had some prior association with the island, perhaps summer vacations, or retired parents living here. It isn't the type of community where there's a job that brings them," states Ann Young, co-owner of Sievers Weavers school and shop. "We're seeing younger couples with children who are trading a city existence for the country. It's not the wallet that's bringing them, but the quality of life."

"When we moved up here the population was about 550," says Munao, who owns and operates the Shipyard Island Marina with her husband Andy. "It's increased by about a 100 people, which is a lot for a small island. A family just moved in, which makes six more students in the school. In populated areas, numbers don't count, but on this island, they do. The school was built for 100; with 110, it's overcrowded."

"In terms of country life, Washington Island is very representative," comments Domer who, previous to being a full-time Washington Island resident, visited the island for 10 years on weekends, holidays, and summer vacations. "You have to do a lot of different things to make a living in the country. The family members who own the Brothers Two liquor store are a good example. Both brothers have other jobs and their mother makes baked goods to sell in the store along with the beer, wine, and appliances."

Washington Island, 23 square miles of fields and forests, sits across from the tip of Door County peninsula, separated by the treacherous and unpredictable waters of Death's Door. This six-mile passage between Lake Michigan and Green Bay, called "Porte des Morts" by French explorers, was perilous mainly for sailing ships. LaSalle's Griffin may even have perished here about 1679. Though numerous wrecks still sit 150 feet down on the lake and bay bottom, today's ferries safely carry passengers and cars across these legendary waters in about 30 minutes.

Washington Island is the oldest settlement of Icelandic people in the United States, many families originally settling here to fish. "The growth of farming on the Island coincided with a huge influx of Scandinavian immigrants, starting in 1880 and going through to 1910, explains Marilyn Domer, a driving force behind the establishment of the Washington Island Farm Museum. In this time, farming replaced fishing.

Most fishermen did a little farming and most farmers fished some—both for their own food supplies."

All the buildings displayed at the two-acre site on Jackson Harbor Road are original island structures. The double log barn, for example, was built by Oddur Magnusson, who also built the Icelandic Castle, used as a rooming house and apartments for the Icelandic immigrants. Look for a photo of the castle in the Gallery Barn, which once served as a 1920s fish preparation shed at Jackson Harbor. Domer talks of the museum's unique collection of historical photos on early island farming. "Apparently there was a business where a photographer went into the country, taking photos of the farms and the people going about their activities. These were then made into postcards and sent to friends. A lot were saved on the island and have been blown up into display pictures."

Wander through the large collection of island horse-drawn farm machinery, some used as late as the 1950s. Forging a link between manual farming and today's large-scale machine farming, these museum pieces were a part of everyday life for the small family farmer making a living on 40 acres with a pair of horses.

"I'm a historian and have always been interested in the part technology played in changing society. Technology in agriculture had a fantastic role in changing our society from a rural into an industrialized urban one," says Domer.

For a while, dairy farming thrived on the island and, in the 1950s, a corporate-type potato farm operation was established, using old ferries to haul the crop to market. But the waters of Death's Door intervened. One winter a boat fully loaded with potatoes sat on the island's east shore, pushed there in a storm.

"At present," explains Domer, "there are only three or four commercial fishing tugs operating and no real farming."

The Washington Island Farm Museum, open mid-June to mid-October, offers live demonstrations and children's activities on Wednesdays during the summer. Special events include an Island House Tour the third weekend in July, the Labor Day weekend Farmer's Picnic, and a cider-pressing party on Saturday and Sunday of Columbus Day weekend. According to Domer, "The Farmer's Union and its followers, as well as the dairy men and cheese-working operators, held a Farmer's Picnic every year. The Labor Day festivities celebrate the past as well as the present, a grand finale to the major part of the tourist season."

"Any island business works very hard for five to six months with no days off," comments Ann Young of Sievers Weavers. "But you know you're going to have the winter. You need it to recharge, to be creative. We see a lot of visitors who come who have no idea why anyone would want to live here. They need their Wal-Mart two times a week, and we don't need those things.

"Because a lot is not provided, we have to come up with creative ideas to entertain ourselves. On Friday night, at the community center's pool, there might be a teen swim with the movie *Creature from the Black Lagoon* shown on the wall. Or on Sundays there might be a spontaneous scavenger hunt with 20 people running around trying to find a photograph of some long-dead relative."

Almost all visitors to the island stop in Bitters Pub & Restaurant in Nelsen's Hall, open since 1899. Built by Danish immigrant Tom Nelsen, the hall itself has served throughout the years as a tavern, movie theater, dentist's office, pharmacy, and ice cream parlor. On the walls surrounding the elegant back bar, brought by sailing ship from Michigan, are early photos of island residents and landmarks. But Nelsen's is most renowned for being the single largest purveyor of Angostura Bitters in the world, according to the *Guinness Book of World Records*. Nelsen himself established the tradition of the stomach tonic, drinking nearly a pint of bitters a day throughout most of his 90 years. During Prohibition, he applied for and was granted a pharmacist's license to dispense the 90-proof tonic to the local residents. More than 10,000 people each year join the Bitters Club by drinking a shot of bitters. Members hail from almost every state and several foreign countries.

Even with a town community center, Nelsen's Hall continues to play a role in island social events. Current proprietors Vince and Penny Jiuditta take pride in their whitefish and home cooking. "The whitefish is caught locally by Jake Ellefson and delivered to our kitchen door Mondays, Wednesdays, and Fridays," states Penny. Penny bastes it with a little clarified butter and a sprinkling of paprika, "baking it fast and hot. I prefer to have the flavor of the fish prevail over seasonings." And indeed it does—indescribably delicious. Both the pub and the Bitter End Motel are open year-round.

Summer visitors discovered Washington Island as early as the turn of the century. Many arrived from Chicago via Goodrich boats which stopped en route to and from Mackinac. That's how Ann Young's parents first came to Washington Island. "Both sets of my grandparents came to the island between 1903 and 1908. One set lived in St. Louis, so they would take the train to Chicago and get on the Goodrich boat. When they would arrive in Washington Harbor, everyone would flock down there. The first frame house in Door County, called the White House, was a Washington Island lodging. The boat wouldn't arrive necessarily at a specific time. If it arrived late in the day, families going to a cottage on the island would stay overnight at the White House.

"My mother was born unexpectedly in 1916. She was due in September and arrived in August. My grandmother didn't have any baby clothes with her, so all the ladies of the island gathered together a little layette."

Today students from across the nation and the world arrive at Sievers School of Fiber Arts to learn loom weaving, basket making, quilting, and garment making. The school, started in

1979, offers nearly 60 classes from mid-May through October, attracting more than 600 students to its weekend and five-day workshops. Class participants find the tranquil island setting a source of quiet and inspiration.

Ann Young explains the story behind this unique island business. "Walter Schutz came to Washington Island when he was 70 years old to retire. Having worked in advertising and sales promotion, he was the kind of man who ran with his dreams and ideas. His wife had learned to weave in Beloit where they had lived. He had always liked the way his wife's maiden name, Sievers, rhymed with 'weavers,' and so decided to design a loom based on the different ones his wife had used over the years.

"Looms on the market at that point were pretty minimal, with not many made in the United States. He designed a loom and started selling plan sheets in 1973, advertising in magazines like *Better Homes and Gardens, Ladies Home Journal* and *McCalls.*

"The looms sold very well, but then he started to get inquiries. 'I like the loom, but I'm not a builder. Do you have a kit?' So, Walter put a little 3″ × 5″ card at the grocery store here, asking if anyone on the island wanted to get into the loom business. He would contract with the builder and he, Walter, would do the advertising and marketing."

Young continues, "My husband and his brothers were just starting a little construction and woodworking business, so they responded. At that time, it was hard to find a loom for the size we were building for under $1,000. But because we cut our own logs and did everything ourselves with no middlemen, we could sell the looms for $485.

"When my husband started building looms, I was hanging around and packing them, but I didn't know the difference between a wire heddle and a reed. Walter said to me, 'We're going to teach you to weave so you'll know what you're doing.' So, I learned and loved it and couldn't weave fast enough.

"Once the loom kits went on the market, Walter started to get inquiries from the customers who bought the kits as to where to go to learn. It was not easy to find a place to learn how to weave. Some technical schools or an art program through a high school might offer a class on a little table loom. But learning how to weave a rag rug, or fabric, or placemats, or lace—that was known by a group of women who were weavers, but they weren't sharing.

"All Walter needed was for someone to say, 'where do I go to learn?' for him to run with the idea. If you teach people how to use your equipment, you're going to sell more. In 1979, the 1896 one-room Jackson Harbor schoolhouse became Sievers School. The first year we had seven teachers and 33 students and taught weaving, spinning, dying, and stitchery."

At Den Norsk Grenda on the Main Road, there are two Norwegian buildings, a single-story *hytte* (cottage), and a two-story *stabbur* (storage building), used as a gift shop. Here, Sievers displays and sells fiber arts and fine crafts like baskets, jewelry, rugs, and clothing made by the instructors and students at the school. Ann's husband Howard continues to manufacture the loom kits from birch or cherry, though the wood is no longer from the island. He does all the work himself, selling as many as 200 or as few as 30 in any given year.

But the school and loom business needs another business to help support the Youngs through fluctuating times in the marketplace. Modular units for model railroad builders, which also were Walter's idea, fulfill that role according to Ann. "His two sons had a model railroad as children, and back in 1952 Walter even wrote an article about modular units for model railroad displays. When his sons, 10 years apart in age, were in their mid-forties and mid-fifties, they decided to revive the idea and put it on the market. They were en route to the island to meet with their father to put the project in gear when they both were killed in the same car accident. But Walter took a negative and turned it around and promoted the idea. It's simply modular framing tables that can be bolted together in various configurations. The units, sold all knocked down with assembly hardware included, are easy to assemble for any size layout and any gauge track.

"Three years before Walter died in 1990, my husband and I bought the business, with him there to encourage and help us. I think Walter knew all along where he was guiding us. We were just naive and having a good time being able to live on this island. We both grew up on the island. My husband worked on the potato farm when he was a teenager, but always enjoyed wood and building."

Repeat enrollment in the Sievers courses is high, and some students have returned every year for a course. Half of those who participate use the dorm in a renovated barn across the street. Others, who may be accompanied by family, find accommodations in an island cottage, motel, B&B, or campground.

Over the years, the existing teachers have found other teachers to add to the roster. "They don't want anyone to tarnish what they've helped create," comments Ann, "so we can't help but get better. Teachers here need to know their craft and how to teach. They also have to have a personality that is warm, caring, nurturing, giving a pat on the back when needed. Many returning students come back for only one teacher. They are almost groupies at this point. It's a wonderful compliment."

Hanging throughout the studio is artwork by various teachers. A small section of the studio is set aside as a greeting area and holds a loom which visitors are encouraged to try. There's also a small store with weaving and craft books plus supplies, including Washington Island wool. "There's not really a tradition of sheep on the island. Most who raise them have moved to the island and want a little hobby farm.

We can't carry completely local handspun because all the prices would be $18 a skein instead of $5," explains Ann.

Though Sievers sells both floor and table looms, all classes are taught on the floor loom. "Looms have to be threaded accurately. If not, there's not an even pattern," says Ann. "It's a little bit like a computer. You have to program it to make it do what you want."

Across from the stone Trinity Lutheran Church on Townline Road (Route #1, Box 208, Washington Island, WI 54246) is a new community project, a wooden *stavkirke* (stave church). "It's absolutely the best treasure this island has ever had," states Ann Young. "The idea came up about 20 years ago to do something like this. Based on Norway's Borgund stave church, it's all locally built by volunteers using pine logs donated by people on the island. There's so much handwork—the shingles, for example, have all been hand cut for the roof. The master carpenter is my brother, John Herschberger, and I'm so proud of him."

Stavkirke

About 33 stave churches survive today from the 11th century, 30 in Norway, and one each in Sweden, Poland, and England. The unique architecture of the stave church blended ancient Norse tradition with the new form of Christian beliefs being introduced into Norway. The originals were very dark, treated with pine tar or creosote to make them black. Two *stavkirke* replicas exist in the United States, one in the Dakotas and another in nearby Bailey's Harbor in Door County.

Planning for the Washington Island chapel began as far back as 1986. A temporary shell was erected around it during construction so that work could continue in all kinds of weather, with the interior warmed by a wood-burning stove. "At first I didn't understand why it had to be hidden under a shell, but now, after all these years, it was like opening a present," says Ann, relating how the shell was removed during the island's 1995 annual summer Scandinavian festival.

An explanatory brochure reads: "Construction of a stave church recalls shipbuilding technique. From the 'stavs,' or masts, of vertically placed timbers, to the arches, or ribs of the rafters; from the finer features of joinery and brackets, to the dragon heads at the 'prows' of the gabled roofs; the wooden structure breathes and lives like a Viking ship."

Jens Jacobsen, who raised his family on the island, wrote poetry, did a little farming, and eventually built a cabin next to Little Lake. The logs were placed vertically because they weren't big enough to do it "Lincoln" style, and the rain would run right down. Near the cabin, Jacobsen set up a little museum to exhibit natural and historical artifacts of the area, including many carvings he did himself.

Jim Gau, who always called Jens Jacobsen "Grandpa," first came to the island "as a baby in a basket," recalls his wife Marilyn. Gau's father, who had asthma, would come to the island in July or August and stay until October. Gau lives on the island in a house he and his wife built almost entirely themselves and serves on the board of directors of the Jacobsen Museum. Although he only retired to the island, during his years here Gau has also served on the school board (even as acting school administrator) and done volunteer work with the Coast Guard. Marilyn writes a nature column for the local paper and joins church women half a day every week, Labor Day to April, to quilt. The group of three to ten church women complete about 50 laprobes and 100 quilts in a season to donate to charity.

Of the early settlers, Gau says, "A true islander never builds on the shore. Look at the old-time islanders here. They all built inland. It wasn't because of the value of the land. It was because of the cold wind."

"There's a little trouble getting on and off the island in the winter," says Marilyn Domer of the farm museum. "For people who have to be specific places at specific times, it's a problem. I'm retired, so I can give myself a little leeway. Winters vary tremendously, though it's not much different from Chicago, maybe a few degrees colder."

The usual 30-minute ferry ride can sometimes take several hours or more to push through the ice. There have been times too, when the boat made it to the other side, but couldn't put in at the dock. A few Washington Island restaurants and lodgings stay open year-round for hardy souls who really do want to get away from it all.

Marianna Gibson tells the story of Gibson's West Harbor Resort, one of the oldest on Washington Island and open year-round. "Built as a lumberjack camp in 1879, it has been a resort since 1900. My husband's parents operated the resort from 1947 until my husband Herb bought it in 1970. We were married in 1971 and have been here at the resort ever since.

"Herb's mother Pearl was born on the island and worked at West Harbor Resort as a young girl in the 1920s. Herb's dad was born in England and was working in Lake Forest, Illinois, when he met Pearl. They married and moved to the island after buying the resort.

"My folks owned and operated Hanson's Cottages in Jackson Harbor. This property is now the Jackson Harbor Ridges, and the house I lived in is the Jackson Harbor Inn. Both of my folks were born on the island, as I was. Their parents before them came from Norway and Denmark. When the town was selling the cottages from Jackson Harbor that my dad had built, we moved three of them down to the West Harbor Resort property. These three cottages increased our cottages to five. Along with nine sleeping rooms in the main lodge, it keeps us busy!"

Gibson's cottages come fully equipped for housekeeping. The sleeping rooms, renting for about $25 a day (higher with more than two people in the room), have shared bathrooms (one for men and one for women) at the end of the hall.

Spring, summer, and fall, bicyclists enjoy the island with its flat terrain and lack of traffic, often picking up supplies at the deli in Mann's Grocery for picnics at the island's beaches and parks. In business for over 90 years, the general store is the oldest family-run business on the island. Golfers ride a ferry to the first tee at the nine-hole Maple Grove Golf Course, later snacking on chili and quarter-pound brat dogs at the club's restaurant. Others come to fish or just relax at a resort, as in the old days.

Many visitors take another boat ride to Rock Island State Park (open late April through October) to see Viking Hall and the immense stone boathouse built by H. J. Thordarson, a wealthy Icelandic immigrant who once owned most of the 905-acre island. A primitive park, Rock Island permits only hiking and backpack camping, May 1 to December 1.

Ann Young recommends visitors see the island from Tower Hill on Mountain Road. "My favorite time to go up there is when there's a full moon," she confides. "You can see the sun setting to the west and the moon coming up over the lake. It's gorgeous."

Old-time Washington Island resident Tom Nelsen used to say "Gos de dang it. You are a stranger here but once." Visit, drink a swig of bitters, and find out.

Places to See, Eat, and Stay

Washington Island Chamber of Commerce: (920) 847-2179 (seasonal).

Washington Island Ferry Line: (920) 847-2546 (schedule varies with time of year; open year-round; reservations required January through March).

Sievers Weavers: (920) 847-2264.

Rock Island State Park: (920) 847-2235.

Gibson's West Harbor Resort: (920) 847-2225.

Nelsen's Hall, Bitters Pub, and Bitter End Motel: (920) 847-2496; (800) 400-0208.

8

LAC DU FLAMBEAU

DRUMBEATS AND MOCCASINS

"I always tell people if the Ojibwe ever had 17-gauge wire before the Europeans came, we would have had skyscrapers here." So states Nick Hockings, giving a tour of Waswagoning (pronounced Wah-swah-gah-ning), a traditional Native American village he has built on his own land. Hockings, a member of the Lac du Flambeau Band of Lake Superior Ojibwe Indians, is a traditional pipe carrier and a certified teacher of the Ojibwe language and culture.

Walking through Waswagoning, which sits on 20 wooded acres adjacent to Moving Cloud Lake on the Lac du Flambeau reservation, visitors encounter authentic dome-shaped wigwams, birchbark canoes, willow fishtraps, firepits, even a beaver run. Waswagoning means "place where they spear fish by torchlight." The French voyagers and fur traders called it Lac du Flambeau (lake of the torches).

Lac du Flambeau became a permanent Indian settlement over 250 years ago when Keesh-Ke-Mun and the Chippewa band settled on the lake with its plentiful supply of fish. Here, the natives discovered that by using a torch made of birch and pitch, the light reflected the red eyes of the walleye pike, making the fish easy targets for their spears.

Waswagoning.

"Chippewa is a misinterpretation of Ojibwe," explains Hockings, "as the elders often dropped the vowel off the front and it would come out 'jibwe.'" Ojibwe means "to roast till puckered up," with reference to the puckered seams on the Indians' moccasins. But the Ojibwe often referred to themselves as "the writing people," based on their habit of drawing on birchbark. "Ojibwe," may be spelled different ways.

Waswagoning, probably the best Native American reproduction village in the United States, is now used as a model by other tribes. In an effort to be as accurate as possible, Hockings talked to many elders as he worked on its construction. Before it opened in 1994, the elders even came out for a visit. But, Hockings quickly points out, "no federal money, no state money, no tribal money was involved. This was built on a purely volunteer basis."

The idea for the project had its origins during the controversy over spearfishing in the late 1980s. In the mid-1980s, the Native American custom of catching spawning walleye with forklike spears resumed after federal courts ruled the Ojibwe retained certain off-reservation hunting, fishing, and food-gathering rights from the 19th-century treaties which ceded millions of acres of land to the federal government. When protestors, sometimes violent, criticized the treaty, people came from all over the United States and the world to support Native American rights. On boat landings in the Northwoods lakes, many non-Indians stood in solidarity with the native fish spearers. Often the activists ended up staying at Hockings's home. From this experience, he learned that there was a lot of misinformation about Native Americans people and decided to do something about it.

In the years since, people have continued to come to the reservation to spend a weekend or longer, volunteering their time to help on projects like the wigwams and authentic artifacts now on display in Waswagoning. It's an idyllic setting. A winding path through woods of birch, aspen, spruce, and pine leads to villages where the work of each season is demonstrated. At the first stop, the summer lodge village, Hockings points out the dried reed skirts around the bottom of the wigwams, important for ventilation.

"It appears quite simple looking at them, but it's very labor-intensive to make them," he explains. "We gather the reeds in the late summer and blanch them in boiling water which breaks down the fiber and makes them pliable. Then they have to be dried and turned frequently or they'll mildew very, very fast. Finally, the women, using a rope made from the inner bark of the basswood tree, tie or string the dried reeds together to make the wigwam skirts.

"The birch tree is considered sacred by our people. The bark, cut about an eighth of an inch deep, literally pops off the tree. You won't find a whole bunch of trees that are stripped, because all the bark used here is from trees that were going to be cut. Theoretically, on this reservation, we can't even go out and cut down brush without getting in touch with our tribal council. Many people think we can go out and just cut down trees anywhere.

"Birch bark has two very special properties. It's waterproof and insect proof. So, when baskets, or *makuks*, were sewn together and lids put on them, the food stored there kept very well for a long time. With the Ojibwe on the move, migrating from one area to another, they would often leave caches of food behind. Once the top was sewn on, pitch was used around the edge to seal it very tightly.

"Many people comment about the white being on the inside, because most people like the white on the outside," he continues. "I tell them that's a tourist basket! The most effective storage baskets, of course, are made with the white on the inside and the outer bark on the outside because it is so insect resilient."

Water was boiled and food cooked in kettles of birchbark. If kept full of liquid and out of contact with the fire, they did not burn.

Summer lodges were relatively temporary. The frames may have been permanent, but the people would take the birch bark with them to use on their lodges elsewhere. The large birch bark squares used to cover the wigwams were sewn together with spruce root. Lashing holes were made through the tough birch bark with awls of animal bones.

Moving through the village, Hockings demonstrates willow fish traps tied with sinew, fish-drying techniques, and arrow and arrowhead making. "On the tenderloin of a deer, a strip cuts off very easily and is as strong as any nylon thread you can buy. This material didn't need to be braided, as the strips were twisted together and mixed with saliva in the mouth to form a glue, making the bow strings very strong.

"The woods are a supermarket. But you have to know the habits of the animal in order to catch it, and you have to know the right kind of trap to set for it. Animals are creatures of habit. To find out where best to set the trap, follow the rabbit's route from where it comes out of the brush pile and crosses to the clearing."

Waxing philosophical, Hockings says, "Just as animals are creatures of habit, people start doing the same thing over and over. They get into a rut. It's like a shallow grave. They get careless, and that's why a majority of accidents happen within close proximity to home. We're so complacent about things we've done 1,000 times."

He talks of special flints, obsidian, and abalone shell—all of which came to the Ojibwe by way of trade routes. "Waterways were much different then than they are now," he says. "From my house in Lac du Flambeau in days past, I could have put my canoe in the water, and if I packed a big enough lunch, I wouldn't have had to take my canoe out of the water until I reached the Gulf of Mexico."

"Maple sugar was our spice of the day," recalls Hockings. "It was used on wild rice. It was used on deer meat and smoked fish. It was used on snow and in drinks. This spring I made some maple sugar which I share with people who come through the village. If you are ever being offered something in Indian country, don't say no to it. It's the protocol that when you are offered anything, it's a gift.

"Maple sugar was highly prized. It was almost a status symbol by how much you had so you could share with other families and visitors. Traditional people never did get into making maple syrup simply because there was no place to store it. We went right through that process. It takes about 40 gallons of raw sap to boil down to one gallon of syrup."

Continuing the tour through the woods from the maple sugaring site to the arrowmaker's lodge to the canoe building area, Hockings comments on common misconceptions. "When I was younger and in the military, I'd hear people referring to the Indian as being very stoic and solemn. They had this image of a guy standing, arms crossed, looking straight ahead, with a frown on his face. But it's people who have never been on a reservation or who have never been around native people who say that.

"Native people are very social. Even long ago, there was a lot of joking and fun in the village. One of the games often played in the summer was lacrosse, the grandfather of team sports. The oldest organized sport in America, it was even used to settle disputes."

The unique thing about this game was that sometimes upward of 100 men were on a team, with the playing field at an extreme of 5 miles long, but many times, well over a mile. There were no rules that applied except one—you could not grab the ball with your hands. It was played with a lot of enthusiasm. Players didn't wear any protection, no head gear or elbow or shin guards. Some balls were made of buckskin, others of wood with a hole through them so they whistled through the air. Often a great deal of betting went on, so there might be a whole pile of gold and spears and pelts—winner to take all. Reports say they played across streams and sometimes even around lakes. Because it was a free-for-all, the game took a long time, sometimes days to conclude.

On the tour, Hockings also explains the procedure for making birch-bark canoes from several kinds of wood, with frames of cedar, and seams caulked and waterproofed with pine pitch mixed with charcoal. He talks about the rites of passage—the Moon Lodge for young women and the Vision Quest of young men.

Ojibwe, Chippewa, and Anishinabe are interchangeable references to the same group. According to Hockings, "Anishinabe refers to ourselves when speaking with one another. Literally, it can be translated seven different ways, but the way that I've been taught means 'from whence lowered the male of the species.' In our culture, woman was created first in the form of the mother. The mother of the earth then reached down and took up the clay and formed this pathetic creature, blew life into that shell, and it was man."

Volunteer guides lead people through the village giving in-depth explanations, answering questions, and presenting a Native American historical perspective which often conflicts with traditional interpretations. Hockings himself usually leads school and group tours. Tours take about an hour and a half to two hours, though Hockings readily admits he could spend a whole day in just one area talking about what goes on there. Having welcomed international visitors from Russia, Germany, Japan, Italy, France, and England, as well as most of the museum curators from Wisconsin, Hockings finds the project much more satisfying than he ever envisioned it.

Waswagoning, on Highway H, one-third of a mile from Highway 47, is open Wednesday through Saturday, 10 A.M. to 4 P.M., Memorial Day to Labor Day. Tours start whenever people show up, with a waiting time of no more than 15 minutes. The village closes for rain (but not for just a light, passing shower).

In the winter when the seasonal visitors have departed, the township of Lac du Flambeau has a population of about 2,500, including 1,300 to 1,400 tribal members. The treaty of September 1854, concluded at La Pointe on Madeline Island, established the 144-square-mile reservation, one of 11 Native American reservations in Wisconsin. It sits amid thousands of acres of wild and scenic forests, a section of the Chequamegon National Forest to the southwest, Wisconsin's Northern Highland American Legion State Forest to the north and east.

Wildlife abounds in the forests and lakes around Lac du Flambeau. Watch for loons running across the water to get up enough speed to take off in flight. Back when the reservation forests were opened to logging in the 1880s, the first tourists of sorts were visitors to the lumber companies, who told others of the area's appeal as a fishing and vacation spot.

On Peace Pipe Road in town is the Lac du Flambeau Chippewa Museum and Cultural Center, recently renamed the George W. Brown, Jr., Museum and Cultural Center in honor of an elder of the tribe. Standing on the site of a former lumber mill, the museum displays an outstanding collection of Ojibwe (Chippewa) artifacts, including a 24-foot dugout canoe circa 1745, taken from a local lake. Beadwork, baskets, and ceremonial drums are exhibited, and traditional Ojibwe clan symbols such as the bear and deer are explained. Summer visitors often participate in half- and full-day workshops in weaving, beadwork, moccasin making, and fish decoy carving.

Four large displays depict the life and philosophy of the Ojibwe as they relate to the four seasons. As an example, during the wild rice moon in late August and early September, families camp together, though each has its own part of the marsh to harvest. Wild rice (*manomin*) is one of the four sacred foods of the Ojibwe, along with sugar, corn, and berries. Actually, wild rice is not rice at all, but a grain or annual grass (*Zizania aquatica*) which grows in paddies as well as in lakes and rivers.

During the "milk" stage, families shock the rice, tying some of the rice stalks to mark their specific area and to protect it from poor weather. When it's time for the harvest, one person pushes the canoe through the water with a long pole (paddles would bruise the plants), while another person kneels on the canoe's ribs with two ricing sticks. With one stick, the four- to eight-foot-tall plants are bent over the canoe, and with the other, the grain heads are gently tapped so the ripe kernels fall into the canoe and back into the water where it reseeds for the next year. Wild rice is still gathered this way today. When done correctly, only the ripe kernels fall off, making it possible to return to the same area several times to harvest more rice as it ripens.

Nick Hockings tells how, in times past, no one went out ricing until the elder, or wild rice chief (someone who had been ricing a long time), gave the okay. "Often he would check the rice up to the last hour before giving permission," says Hockings. "If people who don't know about wild rice whack and bend it when it isn't ripe, it's broken off. I've been out on the rice beds where it looks like somebody has taken a lawnmower through it."

He remembered his youth when he used to help his grand-mother with the wild rice. "The rice is brought up on shore and sun dried. It's moved around with a paddle, because if it stays in one place it might get a little moldy. My grandmother used a galvanized tub, stirring the rice in the hot metal with a paddle. Every once in awhile, she'd stop and bite a kernel. Finally, when it was parched enough, it was taken over to the ricing pits. Baskets were set down in a hole in the ground with a hide or a canvas, and it was my job when I was young to get in there and dance on it. Because I was light enough, I didn't break the rice.

"I danced, and I danced, and I hated that job. It seemed that all the other kids were out playing and I was dancing on the rice. When it was done, we took a flat winnowing basket out in the wind. The chaffe would blow away, leaving the clean wild rice.

"When ricing was done for the winter, our ancestors didn't pull the canoe up underneath a tree and cover it with branches. They took it out into the lake, tipped it over and sank it with rocks to the bottom, where it stayed for the win-ter. Underneath the water it was rodent proof; you didn't have porcupines chewing up your gunnels or paddles, and the birch bark didn't swell up. Maybe the ribs swelled up a little bit. When the ice melted, they went out and took out the rocks and pulled up the canoes."

The museum and cultural center is open May through October, Monday through Saturday, 10 A.M. to 4 P.M.; November through April, Tuesday through Thursday, 10 A.M. to 2 P.M.; and other times by appointment. It has a gift shop with native art and crafts by local artisans. Look for jingle dresses at a specialty shop in the Ojibwe Mall. The outfits with the cone-shaped jingles, made from the tops of chewing tobacco covers, resemble elk tooth and cowrie shell dresses of an earlier era. Two Native American artist shows are held in town each year, one in July and one in August.

Immediately north of the museum is the Indian Bowl, site of the regular summer Tuesday night powwows (late June through August). Here, Lac du Flambeau Ojibwe, in feathered and beaded outfits, dance to traditional drumbeats and songs. Unlike ceremonial powwows where no photos are allowed, this show is based on cultural interchange, so visitors with cameras and camcorders are welcome on the field as long as they don't get in the way of the dancers. During some dances, the audience is even invited to join in. Snacks like Indian "tacos" and fresh fry bread are available.

The Bear River Powwow, an annual intertribal gathering at Bear River Powwow grounds, attracts several thousand Native Americans for three days the second weekend of July. As much a gathering of family, friends, and community as it is of dancers and singers, it's a proud celebration of Native American traditions. The Grand Entry is led by an honor guard of veterans followed by men, women, and children in their relative importance: honored guests; traditional, grass, and fancy male dancers; traditional, jingle, and fancy dress female dancers; and the children by age and dance style. Costumes within each category are very individualistic, with fancy dress dancers always having two bustles.

Strawberry Island in Lac du Flambeau is sacred land for the Ojibwe. "It's the soul of the people, food for the spirit," says Patricia A. Hrabik-Sebby, historic preservation officer and a tribal judge for the Lac du Flambeau tribe. Her mother was a full-blooded Native American Ojibwe, her father, an Irish Catholic. From ages 12 to 28, she sang regularly in the powwow. Now the mother of a grown family, Hrabik-Sebby never traveled off the reservation until 1990 when she made her first trip to Madison, the state capital. Now she flies all over the country, attending conferences and making speeches in her role as the Lac du Flambeau Heritage Tourism Project manager.

Strawberry Island is the site of the final battle 300 years ago between the Chippewa and the Sioux, which expelled the Sioux from Wisconsin. With confusion reigning over rightful ownership of the island, the Wisconsin State Historical Society recently listed it as one of the state's most endangered historic places. Though the Chippewa were given the land in an 1854 treaty, it was later allotted in parcels to individuals under the 1887 Davies Allotment Act. Negotiations are underway to return the island to the tribe to prevent it from becoming developed.

Also in town is the Lac du Flambeau fish hatchery, which raises walleye and muskellunge fingerlings for stocking the reservation's 100 lakes, known as world-record muskie waters. "The eagles like to come to the hatchery for breakfast," notes Hrabik-Sebby.

Just across the highway from the hatchery is the tribal campground and RV park with shoreline sites. Open to the public Memorial Day to Labor Day, it's so popular that reservations are required way in advance.

In fall (*Dag Waagi* in Ojibwe), Lac du Flambeau holds a Colorama Festival in late September. In winter (*Bi Boon* in Ojibwe), visitors come for snowmobiling, cross-country skiing, and ice fishing. As the museum display shows, ice fishing was and is important in supplying Native American families with fresh fish. Winter, in the Ojibwe culture, is also the time for storytelling. Adults and grandparents tell stories about the creation of the world, about survival in the woods, about how children should behave.

Lake of the Torches Resort Casino, on the shores of Pokegama Lake, is one of the few facilities of its kind in the world accessible by boat and seaplane in three seasons and by snowmobile in winter. Though new, the casino hotel has the ambiance of the big timber country resorts of yesteryear. In addition to nonstop casino action 24 hours a day, Lake of the Torches offers live entertainment with top stars like The Commitments, Chuck Berry, Crystal Gayle, and LeAnn Rimes. Call ahead to see what's scheduled.

At Lake of the Torches Resort, you can opt for a whirlpool suite just down the corridor from the slot machines and blackjack tables, or make a 10-minute drive to Fence Lake Lodge to bed down in a luxurious log suite with whirlpool bath, fireplace, two TVs, a VCR, two bedrooms, and two baths. For memorable dining, make a reservation to enjoy Continental cuisine in the rustic charm of the restaurant at Fence Lake Lodge overlooking the lake.

Both Fence Lake Lodge and Lake of the Torches Resort sit on a chain of 10 relatively undeveloped lakes known for world-class fishing. The Lac du Flambeau Reservation offers over 100 lakes for recreational enjoyment. For fishermen, Wisconsin's Northwoods is paradise with its glacial spring-fed lakes brimming with panfish, walleye, and musky. "Wet a line" and take advantage of the professional guide services through local resorts. Join a workshop on surefire techniques for catching walleyes and muskies, or maybe even plan a Lake Superior charter, only one and a half hours away. Area fishing events include Vilas County Musky Marathon (mid-May through the end of November), three walleye tournaments (May), Kids and Kin Tournament (end of July), the World Championship Musky Classic (early September), and two musky rodeos (both in October).

Dillman's Sand Lake Lodge, established in 1934 as one of the first resorts in the area, has been converted to White Sand Lake Condominiums.

"In the 1940s, when it was the custom to have a heavy meal after church, Dillman's was known for its $1.00 all-you-can-eat Sunday lunch," recalls Sue Robertson, who grew up at the popular family resort. She talks about hearing the eerie call of the common loon in the early mornings and the evenings, and of families who returned year after year for the casual, country atmosphere.

Mid-May to mid-October creative workshops ranging from watercolor and oil painting to carving, photography, and personal growth continue at Dillman's former lakeside lodge.

The art program began more than 15 years ago after Dennis Robertson, Sue's husband and president of Dillman's Creative Arts Foundation, attended a watercolor workshop in Door County. Instructors offer quality expertise and are well known, like Tom Lynch who hosted the popular television series *Fun with Watercolor*, and water-colorist Nita Engle. The art classes have been so popular, in fact, that they continue in the off season with Sue and Dennis leading groups of art students and artist-teachers to exotic locales around the globe, from the Caribbean, to Tahiti in the South Seas, to Brittany in France. Both beginners and those with years of experience are welcome in all Dillman's art workshops.

Sue has many suggestions on how to survive without TV: "Take a walk in the woods. Watch the rain or sun on the water. Feed the fish or chipmunks. Listen to the sounds of nature. Pick berries. Look for falling stars and the northern lights."

"There are no strangers here, just friends who haven't met," say the Dillmans. The Lac du

Flambeau Ojibwe concur. *Miigwetch, Ga waa ba min* (Thank you, we'll be seeing you).

Places to See, Eat, and Stay

Lac du Flambeau Tourism: (715) 588-9052.

George W. Brown, Jr., Ojibwe Museum and Cultural Center: (715) 588-3333.

Waswagoning: (715) 588-3560 (June, July, and August).

Dillman's Creative Arts Foundation: (715) 588-3143.

Lake of the Torches Casino: (715) 588-7070; (800) 25-TORCH.

Fence Lake Lodge: (715) 588-3255.

9
HURLEY AND MONTREAL
LUMBER, IRON ORE, AND SNOW

L otta Morgan, Hurley variety actress and lady of the evening, was found in an alley, pistol at her side, murdered with an ax wound in the back of her head—date, 1890! "The day of her funeral the Hurley Opera House was filled to capacity one and a half hours before the service," relates local artist and historian Larry Peterson. "Men in three-piece suits sat on one side of the aisle, working men in grubby overalls on the other. Three pastors, Presbyterian, Methodist, and Catholic, officiated. Eight prominent citizens carried her casket. Out of respect, no 'hooch' was served for one hour."

According to Peterson, "Lotta, with a set of rooms directly across the street from the Iron Exchange Bank, had said she could see everything going on inside. Called to testify for the defense in a bank heist, she disappeared, mysteriously reappearing when the controversy died down. Was she a Pinkerton plant, perhaps?"

Lotta is but one of many colorful figures in Hurley's turbulent past when it was a hot, fast town for loggers, miners, and hunters. On walking tours of Silver Street's bars during the annual Iron County Heritage Festival, Peterson reels off tales about Liver Lip Lil, One-Eyed Mollie, Boxcar Mary, Irish Annie, and John Sullivan with his metal nose. All breathe mystery into Hurley history. And, notes Peterson, "many homicides, not just Lotta Morgan's, are riddles filled with question marks."

Hurley's Silver Street, once the most infamous thoroughfare in Wisconsin, is now the "Life of the Northwoods." Readers of *Snowgoer* magazine have voted Hurley No. 1 for nightlife three times. John F. Kennedy campaigned for the presidency here, where boisterous saloons and "variety clubs" once provided entertainment for miners and lumberjacks.

World-famous Sarah Bernhardt; Edwin Booth, brother of John Wilkes Booth; and Gilda Gray of the silent movie era performed in Hurley theaters. Harry James, John Conlee, and Tommy Cash, plus hundreds of other entertainers moving up and down the career ladder also appeared through the years in Hurley.

Along Hurley's Lower Block, street-level stores often fronted bootleg operations, while second-story levels offered "sleeping" rooms and basements offered gambling. So says Peterson, an area resident fascinated by Hurley's spicy past. The area served as the setting for the movie *Adventures of a Young Man*, about Ernest Hemingway's boyhood in the Upper Peninsula. And here Edna Ferber researched the lives of lumbermen and saloonkeepers for her novel *Come and Get It*.

There are no longer 80 taverns within the space of a few blocks as there used to be. Some still do exist, with their mirrored walls, mammoth polished wood bars carved from gigantic trees, and solid mahogany pillars like those at

Mahogany Ridge Saloon. Lumbermen liked to tell their wives they were going to be at Mahogany Ridge because it sounded as if they were hard at work in the woods!

Visit the Bank Club Bar & Grill in a former bank where the kitchen is in the vault. Drop in at Freddie's Old Time Saloon and Hall of Fame, the Iron Nugget, and Sneakers Bar and Grill in the flatiron building. There's plenty of memorabilia to be found. Look for a photo that appears to be a high school class posing with a teacher, actually the sheriff in a 1942 raid. Periodically Hurley sponsors a costumed tavern tour with characters dressed as miners, loggers, ladies of the evening, and very tasteful burlesque show complete with live singers and stage talent. There's even a make-believe raid on one tavern, set up to include a "front" selling moonshine liquor. Contact the Hurley Chamber of Commerce or Iron County Development Council for details and dates.

Like Iron County, Hurley's past is rooted in natural resources, but its present is firmly anchored in snow. Located in the Lake Superior snowbelt, Hurley's a natural winter wonderland with over 200 inches of snow a year. One of the country's top 25 snowmobile vacation destinations, Hurley has over 450 miles of snowmobile trails, including 50 miles of express riding. Many trails follow abandoned railroad grades, never far from food, lodging, and repair facilities. The Iron Horse Trail, for example, is wide, flat, and easy to ride as it follows the railroad grade formerly used by the Chicago Northwestern Railroad. Once the major transportation link into Iron County, tons of iron ore moved across this route to the Ashland ore docks for transport by ship to eastern steel mills.

Through linkups with other major snowmobiling systems, the snowmobiler has access to more than 2,000 miles of trails, including Ontonagon in Michigan and Wisconsin's Eagle River, site of the annual world championship snowmobile derby and Klondike Days (the most diversified winter event in the state). The old Highway 51 trail leads to Minocqua where one of the bars is in a hotel once owned by Ralph Capone, brother of infamous Al. Northern Wisconsin has the best snowmobile trails and the best trail signs in the United States and Canada, according to a readers' poll by *Snowgoer* magazine.

With 20,000 miles of interconnected snowmobile trails, Wisconsin's a leader in a sport it invented. Back in 1924, Carl Eliason of Sayner built the first machine-powered sled using part of a Model T radiator, a Johnson outboard motor, two bicycle chains, and two sets of skis. Three years later, he manufactured 40 of them. Today more than 2.5 million snowmobiles travel around North America, with nearly nine million people enjoying the winter activity.

The Red Light Snowmobile Rally, the earliest snowmobile event of the season (the second weekend in December), features four days of trail rides and poker runs, plus free guided snowmobile tours. Big Snow Fest follows in mid-January and the Northwoods Challenge Enduro Snowmobile Race is the last Saturday in February.

Ski nearby Whitecap Mountain with its 35 downhill runs, plus "the best mogul runs in the Midwest," according to a Michigan skier. It's a "western mountains" skiing experience at a fraction of the cost, states *Ski* magazine. The resort sits astride the Penokees, one of the earth's most ancient mountain ranges, which once pushed higher than the Rockies and the Alps. Penokee is a corruption of the Chippewa word *Biwabik*, meaning "iron."

For Alpine skiers, it's ski heaven with several other major resorts just across the border in Michigan's Upper Peninsula, and the highest man-made ski-flying hill in the western hemisphere 15 miles from Hurley at Copper Peak. The close proximity makes it possible to ski a different area each day of the week.

Nordic skiers enjoy a vast network of cross-country ski trails, with the Montreal Trails passing by remnants of the Montreal Mining operation, and the Uller Trail winding 19 miles through the Penokee mountain range. Try windskiing across a snow-covered field or frozen lake, or put on cross-country skis and hitch up behind one or two sled dogs to sample skijoring.

For nonskiers, there are plenty of fun winter activities like snowboarding, tobogganing, snowshoeing, and ice fishing.

An Andrew Carnegie/Rockefeller prototype, John E. Burton was an early Hurley entrepreneur, according to Larry Peterson. Burton held silver and gold mine investments in 26 mines around the country and owned a large farm outside Lake Geneva, with 1,000 Shetland ponies and even some excursion boats. Early on, he bought up lots in Hurley, selling them in 25-foot sections, making many of the buildings in town very narrow indeed. By 1886, he had opened the huge 110-room Burton House, known as "the hotel with 1,000 windows." It stood across from today's Liberty Bell Chalet, popular with locals and visitors for Italian meals and pizza. In 1897, Burton sold the hotel for $23,000 in postal stamps plus $7,000 in cash.

From 1880 to the mid-1960s, red gold (iron) was mined from Wisconsin's Penokee range, with 45 of the 70.7 million tons of iron ore produced in this area coming from the Cary Mine near Hurley and the Montreal Mine in Montreal. Shipped to Gary, Chicago, Cleveland, and Pittsburgh, this was the ore that helped build America.

The mines were forced to close when the steel industry changed from using high-grade iron ore from deep shaft mines to using abundant taconite ore economically mined from open pits. Before the mines closed, area residents were earning their livelihoods by mining from the world's deepest iron ore mine, nearly a mile down inside the earth. The last standing headframe in Wisconsin can still be seen near

Pence where the Plummer Mine used to be. The 80-foot-tall device lowered miners underground and hoisted up loads of iron ore.

Other remnants of Hurley's mining past are seen in the giant, pyramid-shaped piles of waste rock tailings near Gile Falls, and the art deco architecture of the Cary Mine Building on Ringle Drive. The Hurley Travel Information Center, at the corner of Highways 51 and 2, pays tribute to the miners with a mini museum. Enormous cores, weighing several tons, sit outside this unique wayside stop. Inside, photos, rock samples, and a miner dressed in authentic garb await the curious visitor. Many of the artifacts were donated by families who had relatives who worked in the more than 350 mines that once operated in the area.

Nearby Montreal, with its 1920s-era white frame houses and gently curving streets, is a former mining company town built by Oglebay-Norton & Co. Actually, Montreal is made up of two distinct communities: Gile on the east bank of the Montreal River, which started as a lumber town in the 1880s, and Montreal on the west bank.

Set amid Montreal's 100-plus homes was the Hamilton Club, the recreational center for mine employees. There was a city hall and jail, a mine superintendent's house, and a mining company office. A landscaping plan supervised by a company-owned nursery employee suggested vines, costing 25 cents each, for beautification and to "gently but firmly eliminate unattractive structures and enhance the general appearance of outbuildings and fences." "Investigations by mining companies," states Cathy Techtmann, community resource agent in the Iron County Extension Office, "had shown that if workers were kept happy, production would remain stable and worker turnover rates could be kept low." The vines have outlasted the mine, with many still visible today.

The Inn B&B, located at 104 Wisconsin Avenue and owned by Doree and Dick Schumacher, is in the refurbished Montreal mine company office where weekly paychecks were once collected by miners and their wives. Doree tells guests about the town's history. Before going skating, children would go to the clinic and get aspirin and cough syrup. Every five years, the houses were repainted inside and out, and all the bathrooms and bath accessories were the same. Rents, at $1.50 per room per month, ranged from $12 to $13 (with a garage), to $14 (if the clinic was used). Driveways were at the rear with separate garages on an alley.

The Inn has a three-story vault, now with a first-floor bathroom inside! The second floor was formerly the engineering department, and the third floor the chemistry lab, still with the original lab table and sink. In addition to three suites, one with a loft perfect for families, the Inn has a sauna. Doree and Dick moved here as retirees for the great skiing, so they are well acquainted with the area.

The Inn sits in Montreal's National Historic District, where the houses are still painted the traditional white. Join a walking tour during Iron County's annual Heritage Festival, or just poke around on your own.

To learn about the history of iron mining as told by the area's architecture, follow the Penokee Iron Range Trail. Take Highway 77 from Hurley through Montreal and Pence to the Plummer Mine. In Pence, note the numerous unique log buildings, built as small barns and garden sheds by early Italian and Corsican settlers.

The story of Hurley's past—its mining, logging, and farming eras—is also told in three floors of exhibits at the Iron County Courthouse Museum. Watch volunteers weave rag rugs on turn-of-the-century looms. The finished rugs sell for about 35 cents an inch, helping to fund the local historical organization.

Local residents touring the museum often point out a father's shaving mug or a sister's graduation shoes. Others may relate tales of their Finnish heritage. Finnish settlers, like many of the area's residents, often worked in the mines and had a farm on the side. After a full day's work, the father would walk the five miles or so to the farm, work the fields, and carry home a sack of potatoes. Usually the mother went out with the children to milk the cow during the day.

The Finns brought saunas to the Northwoods which they constructed from what was readily available, sometimes using even discarded dynamite boxes. In this part of Wisconsin, it's still a tradition to have guests over for a beer, a meal, and, sauna. Hurley's Paavo Nurmi Marathon and Relay, named after a 1920s distance runner, honors the town's Finnish heritage and takes place the second Saturday in August. The oldest marathon in Wisconsin, this 26-mile, 385-yard run is reputed to be one of the toughest in the nation.

At Little Finland, the National Finnish American Cultural Center (U.S. 2 West), see an authentic homestead, buy traditional Finnish gifts, and join in special celebrations throughout the year. Note that the structure is made of timbers notched together in a "fishtail" construction, a unique Finnish technique. For more details on Finnish culture today and yesterday, look for two Finnish-related publications, one in Finnish and one in English, published in nearby Superior. And keep a sharp ear out for uniquely Finnish sayings like *Se on niinkun ahventa takaperin nielisi* (It's like swallowing a perch backward).

Five miles south of Hurley is Wisconsin's only barn made of massive field stones. Listed on the National Register of Historic Places, it was built by Finnish Matt Annala, a master stonemason.

Early farmers in the Hurley area not only had the stones to contend with, but stumps left by the loggers too. A county agent wrote in his report back in 1922, "Stumps proved to be the worst obstacle for farming, 160 boxes of dynamite, some 8,000 pounds, were needed to blast them out of Herman Crego's farm in the Wall Street area of Saxon."

From the 1870s until the early 1900s, giant stands of dense virgin pine over 100 feet tall were cut. Rivers served as the highways to float the logs to sawmills to be made into boards, shingles, and lath for the growing Midwestern markets. Today's canoers often see deadheads (submerged logs left behind) and remnants of logging dams, both reminders of a bygone era.

Canoe/kayak routes in Iron County include the Manitowish River and Bear River (novices); Turtle River (intermediate); Turtle-Flambeau Flowage (lake paddling); North Fork Flambeau River (intermediate/expert); and Montreal River–West Branch (expert), where the world's best youth paddlers, aged 15 to 18, participated in the 1994 Junior World Kayak/Canoe Championships.

The hardwoods did not float like pine but were cut and transported over land once the railroads reached the north. Logging camps dotted the woods from the 1920s until just after World War II. Workers' wages in 1933, according to Cathy Techtmann, who researched logging history for an Iron County centennial book, "were 27 cents an hour working a 48-hour week." At first, logging was done primarily in the winter, with logs floated downriver during the rush of water in the spring thaw, but the railroads made it possible to log and transport timber year-round. Once the Northwoods had been denuded, loggers looked to other ways to make a living. Some turned to tourism, others to mining and farming.

Hurley, along Wisconsin's northern coastline, lies on the route of the Lake Superior Circle Tour—1,300 miles of coastline travel in Wisconsin, Minnesota, Michigan, and Ontario, Canada. Marked with green and white Circle Tour signs, it's part of a Great Lakes Circle Tour that circumnavigates all five Great Lakes and the St. Lawrence Seaway.

But long before the white men arrived on Lake Superior's shores, the Flambeau Trail followed the Montreal River, one of a handful of the world's rivers that flow northward, from Lake Superior to the continental divide where canoes were stored for paddling south to Lac du Flambeau. This route for Native Americans and later for voyageurs, fur traders, and settlers, was the easiest way to cross the dense North-woods forests between the Lake Superior and Mississippi watersheds. It connected two important Native American settlements, La Pointe on Madeline Island and Lac du Flam-beau. Cathy Techtmann likens this historic route to the "Chicago Loop of the time, or the I-43 interchange."

"North of the Continental Divide, unnavigable rivers flowed north to Lake Superior, making travel by canoe impossible," stated Techtmann in an introduction to partic-ipants in a 1994 trek that recreated the route for the first time in over 110 years. "On this section of the trail, all goods had to be portaged 45 miles overland. South of the Divide, just north of Long Lake, navigable rivers flowed south, offering easier water transportation routes into the . . . Northwoods.

"Upon landing at the mouth of the Montreal, supplies and trade goods to be carried on the Flambeau Trail were bro-ken down into packs weighing 80 to 90 pounds, with each man carrying two packs.

"The Flambeau Trail was called a '120 pause' portage, so named for the number of times the voyageurs had to stop to rest. Each pause came about once every half-mile. Depend-ing on the load and the motivation of the travelers, the Flam-beau Trail took between two and a half to seven days to complete.

"Raddison and Groselliers may have been the first non-Indians to set foot on the Flambeau Trail and in Iron County.

In 1661, they reported that they followed their Chippewa guides south from Lake Superior along the Flambeau Trail 'to win the shortest way to their nation at Lac du Flambeau.'"

Francois Malhoit, a 28-year-old clerk assigned to oversee operations for the Northwest Fur Trading Company at Lac du Flambeau, wrote in his journal in 1804: "28th Saturday. I started this morning from Lake Superior with seven of my men to proceed to Lac du Flambeau. I took with me a bale of merchandise, a roll of tobacco, 20 pounds of bullets, three-quarters of a sack of corn, a barrel of rum double strength, and all my baggage. Today we did 40 pauses."

Malhoit's journal indicates that he received animal skins of all types, bear meat for grease, and moose muzzles from the Native Americans. In exchange, he traded items such as blankets, bullets, powder, scarlet leggings, silk handker-chiefs, porcelain beads, "carrots" of tobacco, cloth, and even sleigh bells.

After descending from the Continental Divide, a variety of water highways could be taken. Travelers like Malhoit, who wanted to go to Lac du Flambeau, had to leapfrog from Echo Lake, paddling and portaging from Little Turtle Lake (Grand Portage Lake) to Mercer Lake and finally to the Manitowish River, then upstream to Lac du Flambeau.

Retrace the steps of the voyageurs and fur traders from La Pointe on Madeline Island to Lac du Flambeau by partici-pating in the annual Flambeau Trail Trek the first week in August. Bike, hike, or paddle a canoe or kayak along the 80-mile route on land and water, participating either in daily segments or the entire seven-day guided adventure. Or drive the Flambeau Trail by following Highways 2 and 51 from Saxon Harbor to Manitowish.

Relive the Flambeau Trail voyageur days by attending the Grand Portage Rendezvous, with its shooting matches, blan-ket matches, hawk and knife throws, archery, and woodland walks. The Rendezvous is but one of many scheduled activities making up Iron County's Heritage Festival each year during the first two weeks of August.

Mountain bikers use Hurley as a base to ride the Pines & Mines Mountain Bike Trail system, 300 miles of marked and mapped mountain routes in the public lands of Iron County and nearby Ottawa National Forest. Trails, winding around lakes and past cascading waterfalls, pass through the logging areas of the Great White Pine and remnants of the mining days.

All-terrain vehicle (ATV) enthusiasts know Hurley has the state's largest ATV system, with more than 100 miles of trails. The annual ATV Rally, held Memorial Day weekend, includes radar and poker runs and the infamous mud pit. During the winter, ATVs are welcome on designated snowmobile trails too.

Other visitors come for camping, charter fishing on Lake Superior, and to play the Eagle Bluff Golf Course, an 18-hole, par 71, public course with a state-designated scenic overlook offering a sweeping vista of Wisconsin, Michigan, and Lake Superior.

Hikers enjoy seeking out the many waterfalls located off the beaten path, unspoiled by crowds. Some can be driven to, but most require walking and a bit of orienteering. The 50 waterfalls in the region make a greater concentration than anywhere else in mid-America.

Hurley and Iron County, like Frank Lloyd Wright's home in Spring Green and the Native American settlement of Lac du Flambeau, comprise a Wisconsin Heritage Tourism Area. "Iron mining, coupled with the logging industry, melded the people of the region together and had an important impact on the entire nation," states Connie Loden, marketing coordinator for the Iron County Development Zone Council. "The iron mines of the county fed the steel mills of the nation, providing raw materials for the emerging car industry. The wealth of the iron spurred railroad development and actually changed the course of the rail routes to encompass the iron rich region."

"History seems to be opening many new doors for Iron County and its citizens. I am really proud of the progress that the area has made to use its history as a tool of revitalization and pride," says Cathy Techtmann.

Meet some present-day Hurley area residents at the local farmers market. Amy J. Van Ooyen, for example, is a beekeeper. She frequents the market to sell her alfalfa, basswood, and wildflower honey, plus excess produce from her garden. When asked what makes her so happy, she replies, "I live in God's country."

Places to See, Eat, and Stay

Hurley Area Chamber of Commerce: (715) 561-4334.

Iron County Development Zone Council (ATV, bike, canoe/ kayak, and ski/snowmobile route maps; Flambeau Trail Trek and Iron County Heritage Festival; and waterfall guide): (715) 561-2922.

Recreation report (and 24-hour snow report, November 20 to March 31): (715) 561-FUNN (3866).

The Inn B&B: (715) 561-5180.

10

TREMPEALEAU AND GALESVILLE

STARS AND
THE GARDEN OF EDEN

A rlo Guthrie, Mitch Ryder, Ozark Mountain Daredevils, Marshall Tucker, Steppenwolf, Tiny Tim, Kentucky Headhunters, Dr. Hook, Richie Havens from Woodstock— all in Trempealeau with a population of 1,000! How does such a little town attract these big names, albeit not all at the same time?

"Money," states Bill King, former co-owner of the historic Trempealeau Hotel. "And having it together so they know they aren't coming to a place where they'll have a poor sound system."

Stars Under the Stars features world-famous entertainers from May to September in a unique outdoor concert area overlooking the Mississippi River and Lock and Dam No. 6. Regulars know to bring blankets, lawn chairs, and an appetite. Walnut Burgers—patties made from ground walnuts, onion, three different cheeses, egg, whole wheat crumbs, herbs, and spices—are a specialty item of the hip Trempealeau Hotel. (You can be put on the mailing list for the lineup of musical stars, by calling the hotel.)

The 125-year-old building, one of five left standing when the town burned to the ground in 1888, was moved to its current location by a team of 100 horses, or so the legend goes. Before the fire and the railroad era, the village was located right on the river so boats could pull up and unload. All eight rooms on the Hotel Trempealeau's second floor have river views. Cozy and simply furnished with antiques, they rent for about $30 a night. It's European style (a shared bath) just the way it was in the 1870s. "People who have a bath phobia usually stay at either of the two motels in town," King says matter-of-factly.

Train buffs and families often choose to overnight in the hotel's two-room cottage close by the river and the train tracks. Like most of the historic items at the Trempealeau Hotel, the cottage also had a former life, previously serving as a carriage house for a church. The old building creaks and groans when the wind blows, making it easy to conjure up all sorts of shadowy images, especially when boat horns and train whistles pierce the eerie fog swirling over the misty river just outside.

The Trempealeau Hotel's location on the Great River Bike Trail, which connects with the La Crosse River Bike Trail and then the Elroy-Sparta Recreational Trail, brings people from all over the world. The Great River Trail follows the shores of the Mississippi River, tracing a 22.5-mile path from Onalaska north through Trempealeau and Perrot State Parks to the Trempealeau National Wildlife Refuge. The 21.5-mile La Crosse River State Trail, developed from an abandoned rail line, is a delightful ride along the La Crosse River through farmlands, hardwood forests, and wetlands.

The Trempealeau Hotel's grassy concert area, screened porch, and dining room offer one of the few places on the river with a southern exposure, as the Mississippi River flows in an east-west direction here. Here is a near-perfect vantage point to watch barges and pleasure boats, everything from canoes to cabin cruisers, queue up to pass through Lock No. 6. The hotel's bar, by the way, is one of only about a dozen in Wisconsin that are smoke free.

Come for annual events like the Reggae Sunsplash and Chamber Bike Tour, the second weekend in May; a Blues Bash, the Saturday of Memorial Day weekend; and Catfish Days, the weekend following the Fourth of July.

Bill King was a high school classmate of Hillary Rodham Clinton. King, a senior when Hillary was a sophomore, served on the student council with the First Lady. When the Clintons and Gores were on their cross-country 1992 campaign trek, the Trempealeau Hotel catered a vegetarian lunch for the entourage, including their famed walnut ball appetizers. Photos on the hotel's walls record the historic Bill King–Hillary Clinton encounter. Other photographs record Trempealeau's history and the musical greats who have performed here.

The Trempealeau Hotel's seven-day-a-week season runs "from April Fool's Day to Halloween, or April 1st to October 31," declares King. "I think they should both be national holidays, don't you?" November to March, the Trempealeau Hotel is open Thursday through Sunday.

For year-round riverfront dining, the Ed Sullivan Supper Club is but a short drive from Trempealeau's historic downtown district. "In season, it's not unusual for the Supper Club to serve 700 meals on a Saturday night," claims King.

Not far from Main Street are the ruins of what was once Trempealeau County's oldest brewery, complete with natural caves that kept the beer cool all year. "No one ever messed with the 400-pound brewery owner. At the weekly

Saturday night dances, he'd lift one of his beer barrels to take a drink," recounts King.

Trempealeau serves as a recreational headquarters for western Wisconsin. In Perrot State Park, campsites sit amid ancient Native American ceremonial and burial mounds and petroglyphs. Hiking trails wend to the top of Brady Bluff for panoramic Mississippi river views. The "goat prairie" (a dry prairie on steep slopes), sitting atop the 460-foot river bluff, blooms with little bluestems and purple coneflowers from summer into fall. Back in 1830, when grasses often reached higher than a horse's eye, Wisconsin boasted 7.5 million acres of prairie/savannah. Today there are but 13,500 acres remaining.

French trader and diplomat Nicholas Perrot, for whom the park is named, spent the winter of 1685 here, "at the foot of the Mountain behind which was a great prairie abounding in wild beasts," including buffalo, elk, deer, bear, cougar, and lynx. Trempealeau Mountain, considered sacred by Native Americans, served as a navigational landmark for early explorers. The French name, *La Montagne Qui Trempe à l'Eau*, means "the mountain which walks in the water." Look for its reflection in the bay, especially spectacular when clothed in fall's crimsons and golds.

Perrot State Park and the 6,000-acre Trempealeau Wildlife Refuge, both open all year, are located along a migratory flyway, making them great locations for birdwatching in the spring and fall. Participate in the annual spring birdwatch when members of the Wisconsin Society for Ornithology give guided drives and hikes. Early birds camp overnight in Perrot State Park.

In the wildlife refuge, cyclists and autos follow a route through diverse habitats. Canoeists paddle the Trempealeau River beneath a corridor of trees to Trempealeau Bay, then on out into the main channel of the Mississippi, ending up at the Trempealeau Hotel two miles downstream. Another half-day canoe trip, starting just south of town, leads paddlers through the backwater lakes and marshes of the Long Lake Canoe Trail.

Both Perrot State Park and the Trempealeau Refuge are open for snowshoeing and cross-country skiing in season. "See nature at its own speed and on its own terms," recommends two-time Olympic Gold medalist Andrea Mead Lawrence, a devoted cross-country skier known in the 1950s for her alpine racing skills. "What better way is there to renew and deepen one's coexistence with nature?"

For outdoor enthusiasts on a budget, Trempealeau is a favored destination. Get out in the snow to identify animal tracks. The Trempealeau Refuge and the nearby Upper Mississippi River National Wildlife and Fish Refuge are two of 76 prime wildlife watching sites across Wisconsin labeled with distinctive highway road signs—a white binocular symbol over a brown background.

Some visitors explore Mark Twain's fabled waterway by camping on the water! Houseboats are available for three-, four-, or seven-day rentals, with costs averaging about $16 a day per person on a week's cruise.

For a taste of the country, pick your own strawberries and raspberries, or buy them freshly picked, at The Berry Patch. In the fall, purchase pumpkins, gourds, and Indian corn.

An eight-mile drive inland from the Great River Road leads through apple orchard country to Galesville, site of the annual county fair in July. Snuggled between a lake and a high cliff, this town takes visitors back to yesteryear with its gazebo, swinging footbridge, and horseshoe pits close by the central square. Shop for bulk foods at the Common Market and for sundries and souvenirs at Casberg's, an 1890s department store. Cat lovers head to Casberg's Catwalk, on the second floor balcony, for an array of merchandise featuring cats.

See a two-story New York–style barn and the first upright silo constructed in the United States at the Victorian Arnold

House and Farmstead (open Sunday afternoons, 2 P.M. to 4 P.M., June 1 to early October; other times by appointment).

Inspired by the natural beauty of the hills and cliffs, fields and forests surrounding Galesville, local resident Reverend Slyke wrote and published a theory back in 1869. He matched the area, undeniably he claimed, with the actual biblical Garden of Eden. During October's annual Apple Affair, when the enticing aroma of a 10-foot apple pie envelopes the square, it's easy indeed to imagine this as paradise.

Places to See, Eat, and Stay

Trempealeau County (Whitehall, Wisconsin): (715) 538-2311, ext. 201.

Trempealeau Village Chamber of Commerce: (608) 534-6780.

Trempealeau Hotel: (608) 534-6898.

Perrot State Park: (608) 534-6409.

Trempealeau National Wildlife Refuge: (608) 539-2311.

Galesville Chamber of Commerce (Severson & Assoc.): (608) 582-4328.

11

ALMA AND FOUNTAIN CITY

CLIFFHANGERS

F amous for the House on the Rock, Wisconsin now has a Rock in the House. In 1995, Fountain City made the news when a 40-ton, 16-foot boulder fell 400 feet, partially demolishing a home and narrowly missing the owner. The house, with the rock still in it, was purchased by a local entrepreneur and is now a tourist attraction (open April through November for $1 admission). Stop by for a look at this phenomenon; even purchase some rock-related souvenirs.

It's not Fountain City's first such incident, according to local authorities. Back in 1908, a massive boulder fell from that same bluff, smashing into an adjacent house and killing a woman. Today, that house is a garage.

Sandstone bluffs, often called "hard heads" in this part of the state, make up some of Wisconsin's most rugged topography. Watch for falling rock!

Early settlers here transformed springs bubbling from the bluffs into fountains, giving the city its name. Tucked snugly at the feet of Eagle Bluff and Indian Head Rock, Fountain

City is the base for the dredging barge used by the U.S. Army Corps of Engineers to maintain a nine-foot-deep navigation channel in the upper Mississippi.

Slow down, leave life in the fast lane, and indulge in an old-fashioned ice cream soda, shake, or malt at Lettner's Corner Store at the corner of Main and Liberty Streets (open Monday through Saturday, 9 A.M. to 5 P.M.).

Drive back from the river, taking Highway 95 to Arcadia perhaps, and peer down into narrow, steep-sided valleys called "coulees." Coulee—from the French verb *couler*, meaning to flow—describes these fertile valleys formed by water erosion. A native of the coulee region, novelist Hamlin Garland, wrote biographical stories about the pioneer life of his forefathers here, winning the Pulitzer Prize in 1920 for *A Daughter of the Middle Border*.

In rural Fountain City, just off the Great River Road (Highway 35) look for the Prairie Moon Museum and Garden at S2727 Prairie Moon Road. This 1927 community dance hall, recently restored by the Kohler Foundation, operated until 1955. Locals often confide, "That's where I met my wife," or "I danced all night here."

After farming for half a century, Herman Rusch purchased the Prairie Moon Dance Hall when he retired at age 71. Realizing a lifelong dream, he converted the building into a museum, filling it with area artifacts. Today Rusch is remembered more for his creative garden sculptures which surround his museum. As he explained it once, it all started with a flower planter because the grounds looked so bare. Using cement, paint, pieces of colored broken glass, rocks, and shells, he crafted about 40 outdoor artworks, including dinosaurs, a Native American on a horse, a woodsman fighting a bear, even a bust of himself. His last work, a medieval-style watchtower, was completed in 1973 when Rusch was 88.

Area historical societies operate the museum seasonally, with the Herman Room devoted to this farmer–turned–folk artist. In the off season, visitors view the outdoor artwork from Rusch's red and yellow stone fence with posts like ice cream cones.

For a hearty threshermen's dinner, stop by the Old Time Farm Fest held every Labor Day weekend on farmland three miles east of Fountain City on Highway 95. Watch demonstrations of threshing machines, corn shocking, and silo filling using farm machinery from the late 1800s to 1960.

Merrick State Park, just north of Fountain City on Highway 35, sits along the Mississippi River, its marshy backwaters a home for egrets, herons, muskrats, and otter. Walk Indian Mound Trail along the water's edge, following in the footsteps of Father Louis Hennepin, Nicholas Perrot, and Zebulon Pike, all of whom are believed to have visited the area while traversing the river.

In winter, as in many state parks throughout the state, a night is designated at Merrick State Park for cross-country skiing on candle- or torch-lit trails. Some parks even provide bonfires, lit cooking grills, food, and beverages. Call the park to check on this year's date for candlelight skiing.

Twenty miles north of Fountain City, Twelve Mile Bluff, named by the early river navigators, shelters the community of Alma. Built by Swiss settlers and listed on the National Register of Historic Places, Alma clings to the bluff. Lying 320 miles from Chicago and 100 miles from the Twin Cities and Mall of America, it's just two blocks wide but seven miles long.

Climb the stairways connecting Alma's upper and lower streets to view terraced rock gardens and turn-of-the-century architecture. Browse in one-of-a-kind specialty shops like the Buffalo Trading Company and the Beef Slough

Store. Stop for refreshment at the 1891 Burlington Hotel, (open year-round, closed Mondays) whose owners moved to Alma for the friendly people, slower pace, and no stop-and-go lights. Second-floor rooms above the bar and restaurant can be rented, with reservations, for the night. Nightly specials of steak, seafood, and chicken are offered in the dining room, with a sandwich and goodie menu available at the bar when the dining room is closed.

Drive the steep hairpin curves to Buena Vista Park, on the bluffs 500 feet above the main street and 1,232 feet above sea level. On this natural porch above the river you'll be about eye level with the top of one of the power plant's pollution control towers.

Lock and Dam No. 4 plops right in the middle of downtown, amid waterfront shops and historic lodgings. Use the handy walkway up and over the railroad tracks to reach the lock observation platform. For a special thrill, stand above the tracks as freight cars go whizzing beneath your feet at 60 MPH. Most of the trains coming through will even treat you to a whistle.

Jan Hopkins, innkeeper at the Gallery House B&B just across the street, relates how her husband had a theory about the train whistles: "If the engineer toots during the daytime, he has a girlfriend in town; if he toots at night, he's mad at her."

"I know there's a world out there from what's on the train," she adds.

Jan explained how the turbulence created by the dams keeps the water open throughout the winter for a couple of hundred yards. This open water attracts eagles for feeding, making the lock areas all along the Great River Road a good place to spot the American bald eagle.

Alma never had a depression, as the dam and locks were built in the 1930s. Though river traffic had declined after the Civil War with the coming of the railroads, it was revitalized during World War I when demand exceeded the capacity of the railroads. Commercial river traffic, once revived, continued to grow, yet would grind to a standstill as it had in the steamboat era 100 years earlier when the water level was low. So the Army Corps of Engineers was called in to guarantee a constant navigational water level on the upper Mississippi, building 27 dams between St. Louis and Minneapolis–St. Paul from 1930 to 1940.

Today the heavily loaded barges carry grain downriver to the port of New Orleans, usually coal and oil upriver. A few times a year, the old-fashioned paddlewheelers, the *Delta Queen* and the *Mississippi Queen*, lock through, their presence signaled by melodic calliope music bouncing off the surrounding cliffs.

Jan Hopkins of The Gallery House B&B (open year-round), serves a candlelight gourmet breakfast in a dining room overlooking the river and the lock-and-dam area. "I feel that this could be the Rhine River, or any European river. Every season is special," she says.

The three second-floor guest rooms reflect an English country decor. Downstairs, at street level, the Spice Shop sells sausage and pickling spices and the adjacent gallery has watercolors and photographs, including historical local shots reproduced from glass plate negatives. The 1861 brick building at 215 N. Main Street was the fourth building constructed in Alma. Back in the 1860s and 1870s, when Alma was a major shipping point for grain, it served as Polin & Tester's merchandise store and grain exchange. Quite possibly, lumbermen once bunked crowded together on the third floor of this historic building. Back in the 1800s, Beef Slough, just north of town, was one of the largest log sorting and rafting works in the world.

In Alma, as in other river towns, you can catch a launch to a fishing float in the river. Alma's is the largest on the Mississippi. Whether you spend an hour or the day, it offers complete supplies, including bait and tackle, short-order food service, and night fishing. "Just go to the harbor and post the sign or wave your hands to attract attention," advises Joe Hopkins. For a small fee (about $7) you'll be transported to the float. It's fun even if you don't fish. For early-morning anglers, they serve breakfast.

Try your hand at fence painting, Tom Sawyer style, and sample catfish on a stick during Alma's Mark Twain River Festival every Labor Day weekend. As autumn's blazing colors fade, view hundreds of migrating tundra swans arriving in Rieck's Park, three miles north of town. They usually linger here from mid-October into November or until freeze-up.

Alma resident Donna Krebsbach recommends driving the narrow and scenic roads, hairpinning from the river up to the bluffs. Follow Route 37 along the Buffalo River to Mondovi, for example. Those who want to get out of the car and experience the scenery up close can canoe or tube the river's 25-mile gentle current from Mondovi to Alma, portaging around logs and fencelines.

"I used to own a motel and my tourists just loved it when I gave them those roads to go on," says Krebsbach. "The whole county (Buffalo County) is dotted with century farms, photo ops, and quaint little places. People from the city can't believe how quiet it is. They get out here and want to start following those winding roads up the valleys. They see things that just take their breath away. What the traveler wants, we've got!"

Places to See, Eat, and Stay

Alma: (608) 685-3330.

Fountain City: (608) 687-7481.

Merrick State Park: (608) 687-4936.

Swan Watch (Alma): (608) 685-4249 (early September through mid-November).

Gallery House B&B: (608) 685-4975.

12
PEPIN

A CHINESE PRINCESS AND
LAURA INGALLS WILDER

Over 300 years ago, in May of 1689, Nicholas Perrot, a French fur trader, adventurer, and diplomat, poured oil on the waters of Lake Pepin, lit it, and threatened to burn the entire lake if the astonished Sioux who were looking on gave him any trouble. At the time he was taking possession of all the land west of the Great Lakes "no matter how remote," in the name of Louis XIV, King of France.

Known around the world as the birthplace of Laura Ingalls Wilder, author of the *Little House* books and heroine of the popular TV series, Pepin (on the Great River Road, about 335 miles from Chicago and 85 miles from Minneapolis–St. Paul and Mall of America) now has a new claim to fame: a genuine Chinese princess. Princess Yem Han, a direct descendent of the 12th-century Sung Dynasty, is not only a princess, but a talented artist who has studied with world-renowned masters of Chinese calligraphy.

"Like in the TV series, I'd like to do a quantum leap back to 1127 when Emperor Sung ruled China," says the Princess of Pepin enthusiastically. "I'd say 'Hi, Emperor! I'm your family and I would love to have a one-on-one chat with you about your calligraphy.'

"I feel that it was fate that brought me here," she comments, sitting in her home.

Yem Han moved to this part of Wisconsin in 1990 when her husband, Dr. Larry Hovde, decided to retire and return to his home state. If she had stayed in California, she believes she would still be teaching and would not have been challenged to find other outlets for her creativity.

Growing up in Sacramento, California, Kwong Yem Han (Edna Fong), unlike her brother and sister, demonstrated a natural ability for drawing. When a university art professor suggested she study Chinese calligraphy, she admits she didn't know what it meant at the time. Feeling the pull of the Orient ever more strongly through the years, Yem Han went to Taiwan to study Chinese. There she took private lessons with calligraphy master Professor Li Pu Tong, later continuing her artistic studies in Beijing with Yang Xuan-ting, "the Master of the Big Brush," and Chinese watercolor techniques with painter Huang Xuan-long.

Yang Xuan-ting wanted Yem Han to become "Queen of the Big Brush," and honored her by giving her his special seal, which she affixes to her works in addition to her own seal. "I think I'm the only person who has my master's mark," confides the princess. Of her private instruction with world-renowned Chinese artists, she says, "I always felt that my master teachers were equal to me. When I'm with them, I feel like we're one. I never felt at awe with them, like the other students who would get so nervous. . . . Instead, it was like energy bouncing back."

When she returned to California, Yem Han enjoyed perhaps her greatest honor. The Picasso of 20th-century Chinese painting, Chang Dai-Chien, invited her to his home to critique her work.

While grinding the ink to demonstrate her calligraphy, Yem Han, known as Edna Hovde to Pepin locals, acknowledges she is picky about her equipment. Her brushes, rice paper, ink stone, and inkstick all come from China. "It's similar to people who are gourmet cooks," she says. "Quality is very important to me. It's hard to explain, but I'm not into clothes. I believe fashion comes and fashion goes, but your painting stays. I'd rather spend my money on brushes. I must have over 300 different types—mink, fox, goat, sable."

Yem Han explains how she works. "You have to be really focused. It's an energy that you have. You're kind of in a form of meditation. You hold your breath and go with it. I feel more relaxed when I'm doing it. Time flies."

It wasn't until 1992, when she presented a workshop on Chinese calligraphy at the Walker Art Center in Minneapolis, that her royal lineage surfaced. She had already learned, when visiting relatives in Hong Kong, that her last name was Kwong, not Fong, as incorrectly written by immigration officials when her father first came to the United States. "I'd heard rumors saying that our family was part of the royal family, so I called my father. 'Is it really true, Dad?' I asked, and he said yes. When we were home, my Dad never volunteered the information and I never asked him. If I'd stayed in California, probably the rest of my life I would not have known."

Though Kwong Yem Han has married a commoner, her two daughters are half royal family, which still qualifies them to marry royalty. She has a copy of the royal genealogy chart to show her place in the hierarchy of Chinese royalty.

Kwong Yem Han's calligraphy is original. She does not do prints. In addition she has developed a line of calligraphy note cards. Plates, originally intended only as a gift for her daughters to trace their lineage, are all hand-painted. Priced at $60 apiece, they have proved popular as wedding gift items.

When Yem Han first moved to this rural Wisconsin setting and opened her shop, area farmers who saw her work would say, "Well, it's foreign to me." To relate to her new neighbors, Yem Han began making images of baby chicks. More recently, she has begun doing special commissions, often something personal with an Oriental flair. As the artist herself explains, "I'm moving from the traditional to more East meets West, traditional Chinese calligraphy and painting with Western watercolor and abstract styles."

Kwong Yem Han hasn't had as much time to devote to her art since she found out she is a Chinese princess. "People ask if they can touch me," she says. Some ask her to pose for photos, and still others request autographs. When she visits children at elementary schools, they ask how they too can become princesses. The Princess of Pepin always reminds her young students that today "a modern-day princess has to get a job and work like everyone else."

When Kwong Yem Han added her name as a write-in candidate for the Pepin village Board of Trustees in 1994, she won. She is as proud of that role as of her royal lineage.

The princess knows that her life has been both ordinary and extraordinary. Often she tells this story about herself. "When my husband used to say, 'You must be a princess. You don't cook and you don't clean,' I'd say, 'Don't say things like that. Someday it may come true.'" And so it has.

Today, Pepin is the top international destination in Wisconsin, based on inquiries to the state Division of Tourism. Following World War II, General MacArthur included books by Laura Ingalls Wilder as part of the English language curriculum. Reflecting themes of courage, hard work, and close-knit family ties, Wilder's books have been translated into 40 different languages.

Ma and Pa were married in the area of Pepin, and Laura was born here in 1867. A reconstructed cabin stands today on Highway CC, seven miles northwest of Pepin, marking

Ingalls Wayside

the site of *The Little House in the Big Woods*. The woods are gone now, replaced by farms, with a unique round barn just past the Ingalls Wayside. Yearly, on the third weekend in September, Pepin celebrates Laura Ingalls Wilder Days with a Laura Look-Alike Pageant, parade, period reenactments, craft demonstrations, and horse pull.

The small two-room Pepin Historical Museum (open daily, May 15 to October 15) focuses on the history of Pepin as well as lore and memorabilia related to author Wilder. The Pepin Depot Museum, also open seasonally, displays railroad memorabilia, plus exhibits on excursion, ferry, and logging boats on the Mississippi and Chippewa Rivers.

Each December, Pepin, with the "three French hens" theme, joins with the 12 vintage villages surrounding Lake Pepin in Wisconsin and Minnesota to celebrate the 12 Days of Christmas.

The Harbor View Cafe, at First and Main Streets, draws an enthusiastic crowd of gourmet diners in season (closed mid-November through mid-March). Though no credit cards, personal checks, or reservations are accepted, those in the know eagerly wait two or more hours on weekends to partake of a culinary extravaganza served in casual surroundings overlooking Lake Pepin.

In the off-season when the Harbor View is closed, or if you prefer not to wait hours for a gourmet meal, drive south a few miles to Nelson. Here you can dine on a hearty meal of barbecued ribs or a hot beef sandwich at Beth's Twin Bluff's Cafe, topping it off with an ample slice of their specialty, any one of several fruit or custard pies. Open-year round, home cooked meals are served sunrise to sunset.

While in Nelson, check out the five-generation family-owned Nelson Cheese Factory, perhaps even indulging in fresh cheese curds and the largest ice cream cones to be found anywhere along the river.

Adjoining the Mississippi at Nelson is a huge backwater called Tiffany Bottoms, a sportsman's paradise of forest and water almost untouched by civilization. Trails are not marked and primitive camping is allowed by permit. Contact the Department of Natural Resources at the Buffalo County Courthouse in Alma.

Lake Pepin, 22 miles by 2¼ miles, is formed by a natural dam built up by the river itself when the steep grade of the Chippewa River carries down more and coarser material than the slower Mississippi River can move away. When you look across Lake Pepin today, according to local resident Mike Gleue, group tour guide and owner of Mississippi Valley Tours, it's much the same as when Laura and her sister Mary played on its shores over a hundred years ago.

The natural beauty of the area continues to captivate visitors just as it did William Cullen Bryant in 1870 when he wrote, "Lake Pepin . . . ought to be visited in the summer by every poet and painter in the land."

Places to See, Eat, and Stay

Village of Pepin: (715) 442-3011.

Harbor View Cafe: (715) 442-3893.

Beth's Twin Bluff's Cafe: (715) 673-4040.

Nelson Cheese Factory: (715) 673-4725.

Buffalo County Courthouse: (608) 685-6222.

13

MAIDEN ROCK, STOCKHOLM, AND PRESCOTT

RIVER COUNTRY SAMPLER— BIRDS, ART, AND ANTIQUES

"Maiden Rock has 70 people, but it's booming compared to Stockholm, which has 67 permanent residents. We tend to think of Garrison Keillor's Lake Wobegon as what can happen when development runs amok," comments Donna Krebsbach. A resident along the Great River Road, she works on marketing rummage sales, antique shops, art galleries, and history of America's Greatest Undiscovered Drive.

Maiden Rock, steeped in folklore, takes its name from the tale of an Indian princess who preferred to jump off the bluff rather than to marry the brave her father, the chief, had chosen. Once a site where steamboats took on wood for fuel, it was originally called Harrisburg. Today it is home to the cozy Harrisburg Inn B&B, offering a stereo view of Lake Pepin.

With its 20-mile vista of the Mississippi, sunrise and sunset are equally glorious. In the fall, guests awaken to the sound of train whistles and migrating trumpeting swans. In summer, they breakfast on the porch watching the antics of hummingbirds and pelicans while bald eagles and turkey vultures soar overhead. Here, as one guest noted, it's even possible to commune with nature from one's bed!

The Great River Road, and the Harrisburg Inn's vantage point in particular, provide unique opportunities for birding enthusiasts because almost every type of North American song and game bird uses the Mississippi Flyway as a major north-south migration route twice a year. And the Upper Mississippi River National Wildlife and Fish Refuge stretches hundreds of miles along the river, from nearby Pepin to south of the Illinois border. One couple wrote in the Harrisburg Inn guest book: "We added the prothonotary warbler to our life list of birds." In the summer, look for white pelicans, not often seen in Wisconsin, in the river's pools 4 through 8.

Innkeepers Bern and Carol Crisp Paddock serve up an abundance of warmth and hospitality, taking off for area jazz festivals in their spare time. Feel free to ask lots of questions, as they are well versed in the geography, history, and sites of the area.

With equal ease, Carol talks about the hang gliders who soar off the cliffs at Nelson, fall duck hunters, and the ingredients of the Waterfront Cafe's Bluff Burger (consisting of half a pound of ground sirloin, a bed of crispy hash browns, and a slice of sweet onion, accompanied by a secret blend of "rock sauce" on the side). Bern relates how 18-year-old Ralph Samuelson invented the sport of waterskiing right here on Lake Pepin in 1922. Unable to get up enough speed with a boat, he took off behind a biplane.

If it's scenic berry picking you seek, they'll direct you to Rush River Produce with its six acres of U-Pick blueberries (July); two acres of fall raspberries (mid-August through September); fresh asparagus (May); and apricots, apples, black currants, and garden produce in season. For thrills, they'll send you to the rustic road that crosses and recrosses a trout stream without a bridge! Perhaps they'll suggest canoeing or tubing the 20 miles of the Rush River from Martell to Maiden Rock. It offers a moderate to swift current through the deep, wooded valley, with variable flow and numerous portages. Or enjoy easy paddling with very little current near the Lake Pepin shoreline, staying alert for river traffic, barge wake, and heavy weather.

Carol and Bern will even fill you in about Stockholm, Wisconsin's Soho district, just a few miles south on the Great River Road. Learn all about this early Swedish settlement, visited by Sweden's Crown Prince Gustav and his family in 1939, by visiting the Stockholm Institute, located in the old post office.

More recent immigration in the 1970s brought professional artisans to live and work here. See their work displayed at the annual art fair, the third Saturday in July, and in area shops like the Red Balloon Gallery which represents more than 50 artists and craftspeople. Those seeking investment-quality Amish-made quilts or furniture crafted in pine, oak, or cherry should stop by Amish Country Quilts and Furniture.

When hunger strikes, feast on specialties like catfish cheeks and wild rice sausage at The Stockholm Cafe, home base for Mississippi Valley Tours' step-on guides. You'll find it open at midday, Tuesday through Sunday, year-round (Tuesday through Friday, 10 A.M. to 2:30 P.M.; Saturday, 10 A.M. to 4 P.M.; Sunday, 11:30 A.M. to 4 P.M.). In season, camp overnight at the local park with the waters of Lake Pepin lapping beside your tent.

Prescott, in contrast to the tiny Great River Road hamlets, seems a major metropolis with a population of 3,600. Sit-

ting at the confluence of the blue waters of the St. Croix
River and the muddy Mississippi, it makes a great base for
country antiquing. Begin with the Prescott Antique Mall and
Cellar Antiques right in town. With a map and list from the
local Welcome & Heritage Center, you'll discover that there
are 14 antique shops to haunt in Pierce County.

For a modern souvenir of Prescott's past as one of Wisconsin's oldest river towns, look for coffee mugs designed by
two local artists. Sternwheel steamboats ring the top of the
mug, with the town's historic structures below. Back in the
1850s and 1860s, Prescott's warehouses stocked food and
other supplies for river travelers and traders. A walk down
Broad Street provides examples of the Greek Revival architecture popular during the 1850s.

The St. Croix River, only 30 miles from Minneapolis–St.
Paul, is a hub of nautical activity in the summer and on
weekends in the spring and fall. It is one of the eight original rivers in the National Wild and Scenic River System
established in 1968 to preserve the free-flowing rivers in near
primitive conditions. At the height of the season, yachting
fever is often so intense that the park service has to regulate
the number of boats entering the St. Croix.

Dine at the Steamboat Inn, where the west wall of windows overlooks the St. Croix River and the parade of boats.
For another river view, choose RC's, housed in a former grain
warehouse. Built in 1858, it even had an opera house on the
third floor.

For cider and more than 10 varieties of crisp, juicy apples
just off the tree, visit Orchardview Farms weekends in September, October, and November, or by appointment.

Loretta Richman, a former tourism coordinator for Pierce
County Economic Development, pointed out that unlike
many places in the much smaller communities along the
Great River Road, "all of our shops and restaurants are open
all winter. While it is fairly quiet in the winter, we do have ice
fishing, indoor sports like pool and euchre tournaments, lots

of church suppers, and snowmobiling on 200 miles of trails in the county."

Winter or summer, this whole section of the Great River Road is very casual. "You never need dress clothes. You can travel in jeans and a sweatshirt. That's the way people like it. They're relaxing and don't have to worry about how they look," notes Richman.

Prescott and nearby Ellsworth reflect Civil War history. Dozens of Civil War veterans are buried in Prescott's Pine Glen Cemetery, seven of whom belonged to the famous "Iron Brigade," known originally as the Prescott Guards. Of the 92 shopkeepers, lumbermen, and farmers who left in 1861, 52 were killed or wounded, 27 were killed outright or died from wounds shortly after. Only a handful of the original company was left when they mustered out in July 1865.

Ellsworth is named for Colonel Elmer Ellsworth, pre–Civil War leader of the Chicago Zouave Cadets and the first officer to die in the Union cause. In the early days of the Civil War, his name alone sparked the patriotic fervor of Northerners. After his death, enlistments soared, and poems and songs were written in his memory. The Ellsworth Dairy Queen displays a life-size statue of Colonel Ellsworth and various Civil War artifacts.

At the Co-op Creamery in Ellsworth, buy some tasty, squeaky cheese curds for munching while sightseeing. "By cheese factories and creameries they direct the stranger in rural Wisconsin, for cheese factories and creameries are the most striking landmarks of that country," wrote Frank Parker Stockbridge in a 1913 article for *The World's Work* magazine. His observation continues to hold true even today.

For maple syrup and candy, seek out the S & S Sugarbush, open all year, with a special April open house at the end of the maple sugaring season.

Along the northern reaches of the Mississippi where the Great River Road hugs the river's shoreline, it's easy to forget that in the deep South, levees block water views of the river. To see the river there, even from the Great River Road, you have to look for tall grain elevators, then hunt for a route used by feed and supply trucks to get through the levee.

Karen Lehman of the Prescott Chamber of Commerce tells this story about driving the Great River Road all the way to the Gulf of Mexico. Hopelessly lost in a town and looking for a way through the levee to a river view, she asked some little girls for directions. Not used to their heavy Southern drawl, she barely understood a word they said, but did manage to make out their departing words: "If you can't find it, come back and we'll tell you again."

Back in 1927, Oscar Hammerstein II wrote eloquently of "Ol' Man River," the Father of Waters, in a song for *Showboat*. Follow America's Greatest Undiscovered Drive down a lazy river.

Places to See, Eat, and Stay

Harrisburg Inn B&B: (715) 448-4500.

Rush River Produce: (715) 594-3648.

Amish Country (Stockholm): (715) 442-2015.

Stockholm Cafe (Mississippi Valley Tours): (715) 442-5162.

Prescott Chamber: (715) 262-3284.

Orchardview Farms: (715) 262-3676.

Co-op Creamery: (715) 273-4311.

S & S Sugarbush: (715) 594-3632.

14

MADELINE ISLAND, BAYFIELD, AND THE APOSTLE ISLANDS

FUR, SAILS, AND LIGHTHOUSES

"**I** discovered the area and stopped traveling," says Virginia Duncan, a nationally recognized travel expert and consultant. "Bayfield and the Apostles mean R and R—rest and renewal, where time doesn't matter. With great beaches, great biking and charter sailing, it's a kick back and relax place. It's the only place I know where people can experience the romance of sailing by going to the dock and signing up for a three-and-a-half-hour sail for $40 or so." The authors of *Super Family Vacations* concur, listing the Apostles as a dream spot for family sailing vacations.

"When you get here, you have the feeling 'I found it; I discovered it.' It's already discovered in Door County," comments a Madeline Island summer resident who winters in St. John, the U.S. Virgin Islands.

"People are drawn to the Apostles. They speak to you. The second year when I got my first sight of the islands as I came over the brow of the hill, I thought, 'I'm coming home.' Yet,

I had only spent four days there in my whole life," recalls Duncan, who served many years on Wisconsin's Governor's Council on Tourism.

"Occasionally," says Sharon Johnson, former Bayfield Chamber of Commerce president, "we get these people who say, 'You really don't have a lot up here. What about some water slides?' But we have tranquility and beauty, and you can let your children walk and be comfortable and not worry. There are not too many places that can offer that anymore. We're not neon lights and hubbub, but if you want a nice, beautiful, breathtaking, relaxing spot, this is it.

"When the moon and stars are out, you can take a romantic ferry ride over to Madeline," she continues. Johnson, with her husband John, runs the Bay Front Inn and Pier Restaurant. The Pier sits on a corner where there used to be a little log A&W stand, the charter headquarters for fishing as far back as 1937.

Bayfield, the gateway to the Apostles, claims fame with a National Historic District, numerous B&Bs, apple orchards, and superlative scenery. Lumberjacks, stonecutters, fishermen, and tourists have all followed in the footsteps of the French voyageurs over the years. Here was quarried the brownstone for New York and Chicago. From here thousands of barrels of fish left for major metropolitan areas. And here today is centered the largest group of charter sailboats in the continental United States.

Bayfield and the Apostles make for a unique cruising ground. Beginner sailors never have to leave sight of land. Novices and experts alike easily find lee shores for protection when the wind picks up. Scuba divers enjoy clear, clean water with fascinating underwater rock formations and numerous shipwrecks. Kayakers like to explore the sea caves for which the Apostles are famous.

Sail away for a week or a day on a captained vessel or bareboat charter. In three days, you can learn how to skipper a 29-foot, single-masted sailboat over the Great Lakes. Women often try a women's basic sailing course. Watch or join the annual 60-mile Around the Islands Race, part of the Apostle Islands Yacht Club's annual Race Week during the first week in July.

To many, Bayfield is synonymous with the Rittenhouse Inn, voted "the best bed and breakfast in Wisconsin" two years in a row by readers of *Wisconsin Trails* magazine. When Mary and Jerry Phillips opened the Queen Anne mansion as a B&B over 25 years ago, they sought to "create a place that transcends time." White wicker rockers on a wraparound porch catch breezes from the sparkling waters of Lake Superior. Bounteous gourmet meals, in several courses, are elegantly served. Antique-furnished rooms come complete with fireplaces and double whirlpools. Couple these charms with warm hospitality, and no one doubts that Mary and Jerry have achieved their goal, setting the standard by which other B&Bs are judged.

Jerry talks of taking an early evening ride with Mary through the nearby hilltop orchards in late May, drinking in the fragrance of the apple blossoms. The aromatic memory, he says, helps carry him through the frosty cold winter months when snow blankets Bayfield, often with up to 100 inches in a season. "You can't have spring if you don't have winter," he philosophizes.

From the early years of running one of Wisconsin's first B&Bs, Mary and Jerry refused to accept that Bayfield was a one-season town. They planned special Christmas and Valentine musical dinner programs. Guests seeking the out of the ordinary came, discovering arcticlike beauty in the Midwest.

Winter brings downhill and cross-country skiing, ice fishing, snowmobiling, even dog sledding and winter camping. Take a dog-sled trip through the Apostle Islands and Chequamegon National Forest on any weekend from December through March, traveling five to ten miles a day and staying in tents, snow shelters, or cabins. Or plan a day visit to the Squaw Bay Sea Caves where centuries of wave action, freezing, and thawing have carved intricate sandstone caves. In the summer they're reached by boat, but in winter adventurous explorers can, when the ice allows, walk, snowshoe, ski, or snowmobile to the blue-green ice falls and caverns. Even test your agility in the annual five-mile Run on Ice to Madeline Island.

Residents used to bobsled on Manypenny Avenue hill, innkeepers Julie and Larry MacDonald tell their guests at the Cooper Hill House B&B. Today's winter visitors can't do that, but they can ride a windsled—part boat and part airplane— a flying toboggan of sorts! Perhaps the only contraption of its kind anywhere, it is somewhat akin to a Florida Everglades airboat. Powered by an airplane engine and a pusher propeller, the windsled treks between Bayfield and Madeline Island during the few weeks each year when the ice is too thick for the ferries and too thin for cars or even snowmobiles. Sometimes in emergencies, it even serves as an ambulance. The windsled, a jack-of-all-trades machine, cruises through open water, skims over good ice, and works a path through broken ice.

Gary Russell, of the Madeline Island Ferry Line, indicates that "generally the ferries run until the first week in January, shutting down for about 10 weeks on an average. About half of that time, the ice is thick enough for people to drive back and forth. The windsled has to be much heavier than a Florida Everglades windboat because of the ice hammering the hull. We run the ferry until the sled can go across without breaking through. It takes about six inches of ice. The ferry can break seven or eight inches of ice without too much difficulty. The problem is that the ice never freezes uniformly. There can be eight inches of ice on the island side and four inches over in Bayfield, so we have to wait for Bayfield to catch up."

Ferries have linked Bayfield to Madeline Island since about 1900 when sailing boats were introduced by Gary's grandfather, Charles P. Russell. Elmer Nelson, a member of Madeline Island's other ferry family, developed the first windsled in the 1940s. All have been homemade. One of the very first used a Model-T front end, and another a motor from an army surplus Mark IV tank that General Patton's forces used in North Africa. An early sled was described as "a 16-foot-long plywood-and-steel scow on runners."

Several years ago the two ferry families, the Russells and the Nelsons, merged their transportation ventures into the Madeline Island Ferry Line. It's a lifeline for the 200 or so year-round residents of Madeline Island. When the windsled and ferry are not in use, a line of Christmas trees marks the car route across the ice from Bayfield to La Pointe. Russell cautions that winter visitors to Madeline Island should not drive across in a car if they're unfamiliar with the area. "Follow a local or the guys that plow the road across the ice," he advises.

Bayfield, with no chain restaurants, no Dairy Queen and no McDonald's, does have "the Carnegie Hall of Tent Shows," Lake Superior Big Top Chautauqua. The early chautauquas, based on the first one in upstate New York, "brought culture to people in the hinterlands, to better the mind as well as to entertain," states Virginia Duncan. In 1894, there were 50 such chautauqua assemblies around the country. One hundred years later, the count stood at 33, with Bayfield's modern chautauqua celebrating its 10th birthday in 1995. Each summer, June through Labor Day, under a tent on Mount Ashwabay's hillside, all ages thrill to a smorgasbord of family entertainment—concerts, live theater, humor, and original historical musicals.

"The original musicals are brilliantly written and magnificently executed, with great lyrics," enthuses Duncan.

"They are unique and not to be duplicated anywhere." *Take It to the Lake*, with Lake Superior as the leading lady, commemorates past and present life along the shores of this inland sea. *On the Velvet* takes a nostalgic look at the golden age of railroads. *Riding the Wind*, Chautauqua's flagship show, presents a history of Bayfield and the Apostles.

Intertwined with the historical musical productions are performances by internationally featured artists like Robert Bly, country star Kathy Mattea, Garrison Keillor, legendary folk singer Arlo Guthrie, and the National Shakespeare Company. Here, audiences find the entire spectrum of theater, poetry, and music (from blues, bluegrass, and jazz to gospel, folk, and classical).

When a storm devoured the first tent, a new one was specially ordered at great expense because it had to be canvas. Canvas tents, it seems, just aren't manufactured anymore. But Chautauqua wouldn't be Chautauqua without canvas, believe its supporters. "They tried to take Chautauqua to the public in the winter by doing the shows in high school auditoriums," says Duncan. "But for me, it's not the same unless it's right in the Big Top."

Keeper of the Light, a musical history of the Apostle Islands lighthouses and their keepers, blends stories and journals of the lightkeepers with old photos of the light stations when they were manned. Relive spine-tingling chronicles of Lake Superior storms and haunting bittersweet stories depicting the keeper's lonely life, then take a cruise on the *Island Princess* to see the lighthouses as they are today. From Devil's Island, the northernmost point of Wisconsin, you may even catch a glimpse of the oreboats on the largest freshwater lake in the world. Ranger staff and volunteers, in season, carry on the lighthouse-keeping tradition by conducting tours and helping maintain the buildings and grounds. Some even portray the role of real-life "wickies."

Before automation, head lightkeepers often shared duties with assistants, as lights had to be kept burning from one half hour before sunset until one half hour after sunrise. Fuel oils used to light the lamps dirtied and clouded the lens as well as the windows of the tower, so all of the glass and brass parts had to be cleaned and polished daily. Wicks, too, were trimmed and adjusted every day. Despite the hard and tedious labor and an average yearly salary of $600, the Apostle Islands were a favorite duty station for lightkeepers and their families in the late 1800s. Unlike ocean assignments, the job was seasonal, permitting them to move back to town for a more normal life in winter. And on these islands they not only had land for gardens, but areas to hunt and explore as well.

For an overall introduction to the Apostles, stop at the lakeshore's headquarters in the historic brownstone Bayfield County Courthouse. Disembark from a cruise to explore an island for a couple of hours on your own, touring a lighthouse and visiting a 1930s restored fish camp. Plan an even longer stay by camping on one or more of the islands. To really get away from it all, apply to be a seasonal ranger or one of the 60 or more volunteers who work at the Apostle Islands National Lakeshore. Be a lighthouse keeper Memorial Day through mid-October, spending ten days on and four days off an island. After a season spent in this rustic and primitive archipelago, "you'll have the mosquitoes asking for you by name," according to William J. Ferraro, Volunteers-in-the-Parks coordinator.

In 1995, the Apostle Islands National Lakeshore celebrated its 25th anniversary. Before this beautiful and unique ecosystem was established, former Wisconsin Senator Gaylord Nelson said, "There is not another collection of islands of this significance within the continental boundaries of the United States. I think it is tremendously important that this collection of islands be preserved." Today, as in centuries past, the Apostles appear as emeralds scattered in a sapphire sea.

With more than a dozen islands making up the chain, some say they were named for twelve apostles, seven devils, and two sisters." Madeline Island, fourteen miles by three miles, and the largest of the Apostles, is not a part of the national park. Though the only island with commercial development, it is the spiritual home of the Ojibwe people.

In 1490, Ojibwe Indians came from the east, settling on Madeline Island and naming it *Moningwunaukauning* (place of the golden-breasted woodpecker). By 1671, La Pointe had become the official headquarters for 12,000 members of the Indian nation. When the treaty of 1854 forced the Native Americans to leave the island for reservations, elders hid sacred birch-bark scrolls in the sandstone caves. According to prophecy, someday a young boy will discover these scrolls and the Ojibwe will reclaim their sacred land, reestablishing the grand medicine lodge in the place of the golden-breasted woodpecker.

"They come back and have ceremonies at their little park by the marina," says year-round Madeline Island resident Nori Newago. "The land in Ojibwe Memorial Park was given back to the Indians. Ojibwe from all over Wisconsin come to Madeline. On Memorial Day weekend, they come over to drum and replenish their flag. The flag is red, yellow, and black, representing the colors of the world's people, and then green for the earth and blue for the sky."

The park is also the burial site of O-Shaka, chief speaker of the Ojibwe on Lake Superior and son of Chief Buffalo. Just adjacent, behind the Madeline Island Yacht Club and five blocks from the ferry landing, is the rustic Indian burial ground, slowly returning to its natural state as the Ojibwe tribe wishes. Some gravesites are covered and protected by roofed shelters, miniature houses of sorts used to protect the dead as well as the food left for nourishment on the four-day journey to the afterlife.

In addition to being important to Native Americans, La Pointe was a key in the struggle between France, England, and the United States to control the fur trade. Long before La Pointe became an actual village, it was synonymous for the western part of Lake Superior, where the long winters and dense forests produced pelts that were highly prized by the fur traders. In 1638, Radisson and Groseilliers, often referred to locally as "radishes and gooseberries," began fur trading activities at La Pointe which continued for 200 years. Look for the return of the voyageurs each summer during the second weekend in August (August 13–15, 1999), when a reenactment troupe sets up an authentic French voyageur encampment at the local museum. On another summer weekend, celebrate folk traditions during Island Homecoming, the fourth weekend in July (July 23–25, 1999).

The Madeline Island Historical Museum (open late May through early October), built on what was once the site of the American Fur Company, is made up of four older buildings, including a former American Fur Company storage building and the old town jail. Through the museum's displays on Ojibwe culture, the fur trade, and the arrival of missionaries, loggers, fishermen, and summer tourists, discover the rich tapestry of Wisconsin history. Learn how beaver furs saved France from bankruptcy, bought corner lots in New York City still owned by the Astor family, and caused men to walk thousands of miles to Astoria, Oregon. Was the beaver perhaps Jason's Golden Fleece after all?

For items hand crafted by islanders, visit Woods Hall Craft Shop (open Memorial Day until the Apple Fest), three blocks south of the ferry landing. According to Nori Newago, who now runs her own marketing and consulting firm, "It all started with a minister who wanted to create an industry on the island, as the winters were very long and unprofitable. A lot of people, both men and women, came down and actually earned a living weaving in the craft shop. When I was first here, before my kids were grown, I had to stay home. I did a lot of weaving there. It kind of carried us through the winter." Though woven rugs and placemats are the mainstay, a variety of high-quality craft items in woodcarving, woodworking, basketry, pottery, and jewelry represent the work of more than 50 craftspeople ranging in age from 8 to 93.

Year-round, advises Newago, "you can always find coffee at Ed's Island Cafe. If no one is there, just take some coffee and leave the money."

In the 1890s, people began to discover Madeline Island as a refuge from summer's heat and hay fever. Nebraska Row, a row of houses on the shoreline north of the ferry dock, started when Colonel Frederick Woods of Lincoln, Nebraska, built a summer home in 1899. Woods then convinced many of his well-to-do friends to build here too, among them Hunter L. Gary, the founder of General Telephone.

Woods Manor, on Nebraska Row, is one of the grand traditional summer houses built by the Woods family. Its stucco walls, wooden beams, and wrought-iron fixtures give it a Spanish feel. In the Woods family until recently, the manor has been renovated with exacting devotion by a Chicago couple who stumbled onto Bayfield by mistake. Enjoy *Great Gatsby*-style lodging at The Woods B&B, once an island hot spot for parties, where yachts of the elite lined up along the shore. "My husband Joe and I have had a house in Bayfield," says Lisa Burn, owner of The Woods. "We loved it up here and had to figure out a way to make a living. We believe Madeline Island is on the verge of being discovered."

Play golf at the Madeline Island Golf Club and the Apostle Highlands Golf Course, both with sweeping vistas of Lake Superior. Dine at Maggie's, Greunke's, and the Rittenhouse in Bayfield (all three open all year), and at The Clubhouse on Madeline Island, "one of the top dining experiences our state has to offer," according to the *Milwaukee Journal Sentinel.* Open for dinner Wednesday through Sunday, June until Apple Fest and weekends in May and October, it's worth a special trip. Reservations are needed.

By all means be sure to try the local delicacy, whitefish and whitefish livers. Bayfield is the only place on the lake where commercial fishermen take the time to save the livers. "Whitefish," wrote an early traveler to the area, "is the daily bread of the fishermen. It's most abundant and can be caught the whole year through. The snow white meat has a good taste, and when boiled, it's rather flaky, never dry. You can eat it for breakfast, dinner and supper without growing surfeited, especially when cooked by the Indian women."

For those who want to rough it, both Big Bay State Park (open all year) and Big Bay Town Park are popular with campers. Big Bay has an indoor camp for organized groups, and both parks have one-and-a-half-mile sand beaches, though often it's only children who brave the cold water to swim in Lake Superior.

With dogsledding in winter, sailing in summer, and a fall color season rivaling that found in New England, Bayfield, Madeline Island, and the Apostles have appeal year-round. For over 30 years, Bayfield has recognized the apple harvest with its Apple Fest. Many come to take orchard tours and pick their own, some even planning family reunions to coincide with fall's colorama.

Take in the silent splendor of winter from the comfort of the contemporary Thimbleberry Inn B&B. Snuggled cozily next to the warmth of your fireplace, look out on Lake Superior and five Apostle Islands blanketed in white. A 19th-century guest described the Apostle Islands this way: "It looks like a fairy scene and everything about it is enchantment."

Virginia Duncan still raves about her first Chautauqua experience. "My favorite night of the whole world is when I first heard 'Riding the Wind.' They sang about the early French traders at old La Pointe, and how the lights along the shore looked like stars come down from heaven. After the show, I rode the midnight ferry from Bayfield back to Madeline Island. Seeing old La Pointe and the string of lights along the shore like stars come down from heaven, I thought, 'This is heaven.'"

Places to See, Eat, and Stay

Bayfield Chamber of Commerce: (715) 779-3335; (800) 447-4094.

Madeline Island Chamber of Commerce: (715) 747-2801.

Apostle Islands National Lakeshore: (715) 779-3397.

Rittenhouse Inn: (715) 779-5111.

Big Top Chautauqua: (715) 373-5552.

Madeline Island Ferry Line: (715) 747-2051.

Windsled: (715) 747-3300 (winter season varies).

The Woods B&B: (715) 747-3102; (800) WOODS-56 (966-3756).

The Clubhouse: (715) 747-2612.

Big Bay State Park: (715) 779-4020; (715) 747-6425 (in summer).

Dogsled treks (715) 779-3320.

Thimbleberry Inn: (715) 779-5757.

INDEX